Chicken Soup
Indian Bride's Soul
for the

Chicken Soup Indian for the Bride's Soul

Stories of Love, Laughter and
Commitment to Last a Lifetime

Jack Canfield,
Mark Victor Hansen and
Raksha Bharadia

westland

We would like to acknowledge the following publishers and individuals for permission to reprint the following material. (Note: the stories that were penned anonymously or that are public domain are not included in this listing.)

A New Me. Reprinted by permission of Kiran Manral. © 2010 Kiran Manral.

All for Love. Reprinted by permission of Arti Sonthalia. © 2010 Arti Sonthalia.

Coffee. Reprinted by permission of Joie Bose. © 2010 Joie Bose.

(continued on page 367)

westland ltd
Venkat Towers, 165, P.H. Road, Maduravoyal, Chennai 600 095
No. 38/10 (New No. 5), Raghava Nagar, New Timber Yard Layout, Bangalore 560 026
Survey No. A-9, II Floor, Moula Ali Industrial Area, Moula Ali, Hyderabad 500 040
23/181, Anand Nagar, Nehru Road, Santacruz East, Mumbai 400 055
47, Brij Mohan Road, Daryaganj, New Delhi 110 002

Contents

12. TREASURED MOMENTS

Introduction

The first thing I remember as I opened my eyes on the morning of my wedding day was the lilting fragrance of mehndi and the orange that had turned into a deep maroon as was promised. I followed the intricate pattern all the way to below my elbows and then lifted my feet and admired more of it on my ankles. I smiled. And then I turned sideways to see her sleeping by my side.

My mother had shooed away all my friends and cousins to sleep next to the 'bride' and was still in deep slumber. I knew she had been up till the wee hours of morning making sure every little thing was in place for the big day. Through the entire last week I had not seen her forehead once free of worry lines, and here she was so calm and serene in her sleep. Suddenly a slight chill ran down my body at the thought that after that morning, wanting to wake up next to her would need prior planning.

I heard the phone ring in the drawing room (there were no cell phones then) and knowing it to be from 'him', I ran to get it. 'So Miss Killa, this is the last time I can address you so...' he teased. I blushed and giggled at the same time. As I made my way back to my room of nine years and sat on the little puff facing my dressing table, a feeling of gloom once again shadowed the hitherto 'happy' me. I had approved even the shade of curtains in my so called 'new home' but at that moment the thought gave me no comfort.

And so it followed for the rest of my big day, deep excitement would suddenly give way to uncontrollable anxiety, laughter would replace tears without a warning, hugs would be endless, tighter, conversation either in spurts or stunted and I did not know till then that it was possible to feel 'complete' and 'alone' at the same time...and this is what I exactly felt!

Welcome to *Chicken Soup for the Indian Bride's Soul!* This is rightfully believed to be the paramount time in a person's life and by sharing their emotional experiences, our contributors have captured and brought alive the fantasy of new brides. These heartwarming stories prop up the belief that marriages are made in heaven and celebrated on earth. It is the physical, emotional and sacred harmony of two souls which comes with its own trimmings.

I received stories where the contributing authors have candidly revealed their inconsistent emotions during the period before marriage. The naive bride-to-be is gripped by an overpowering state of happiness along with the pain of leaving her family and home that constituted her identity. She is surmounted with feelings of joy accompanied with qualms about her loss of independence, nervousness about her soul mate being the appropriate choice or even worries about her challenging to-be-mother-in-law causing pandemonium during the wedding. The 'mother-in-law' is always a sensitive subject matter and I have some funny yet poignant stories about them.

In these stories, you will relive the festivities and the exuberance that come as a part and parcel of our big fat Indian weddings. It promises to be an insightful journey panning the multifaceted ethnicity of India.

I have hilarious anecdotes that will take you on an exhilarating rollercoaster ride through the entire scenario of groom-hunting as in the instance of arranged marriages. Reading about love-at-first-sight, bells ringing and, of course, comical faux pas will rekindle some of your own memorable moments and make you smile at the innocence of it all. These stories substantiate that arranged marriages can be extremely exciting and action-packed. Coming to love marriages, I have contributions that will enlighten readers with novel ways of popping the big question and dealing with resisting in-laws. So, if you could do with any such information, you just might stumble on some 'tried and tested' guidelines right here in this book!

Marriage is a life-changing happening for everyone, and the experiences that come along with it always make us more judicious. I have stories with some amazing words of wisdom from immature-turned-wise brides. These soul-stirring stories will make an enriching read for you.

So readers! Put on your rose-tinted spectacles and lay back as you are transported into the idyllic world of brand new brides where everything is almost paranormal. Brace yourself for a whole lot of nostalgia and if you are one of those planning your dream wedding, you will relate to the mood of never ending high in this book. And if this joyride stirs you to pen your own thoughts and experiences, then please do so … and share them with us!

–Raksha Bharadia

1

THE MEANING
OF MARRIAGE

The real act of marriage takes place in the heart, not in the ballroom or church or synagogue. It's a choice you make — not just on your wedding day, but over and over again — and that choice is reflected in the way you treat your husband or wife.

–Barbara De Angelis

A New Me

I don't remember much about my wedding day. It passed in a kind of crazy blur where everything merges into one big whirl of events, incidents and anecdotes that pop up in your mind when you're least expecting it. It was a conventional Hindu wedding. We had the jaimala, the kanyadaan, the saat *pheras* around the sacred fire as was mandatory, the havan, followed by the reception. For me, this was a first of sorts. The first time I had ever participated in a havan. The first time I had sat down before a sacred fire, and heard the chanting of the mantras, felt the smoke rise from the havankund and go into the ethers, to the abode of the Gods, hopefully, all of whom were standing, decked out in full regalia as is mandatory with the Gods, showering blessings in the form of petals down on us, as I had seen in television serials based on the religious epics. You see, I was marrying into the Hindu community. I was born to a Muslim father and a Catholic mother. My religious upbringing was, to say the least, very sparse. I had done the occasional trips to the church in my childhood, my mother had continued with her religion after her marriage as had my father with his, and neither had infringed upon each other's choice of religion.

I had grown up like a weed, with no religion, but with knowledge of every religion. I was a voracious reader and had studied the Gita, the Upanishads, the Koran, the Guru Granth Sahib, the Bible and even the Torah. All in translation of course, and I knew that God, through whatever route one took to Him, was the same across all religions.

But, I was marrying a man I had loved with all my heart and soul for the past six years. And he was a Hindu. And a very religious person. He went every Tuesday to Siddhivinayak Mandir at Prabhadevi and I accompanied him when I could. To be fair, he also visited the Haji Ali Dargah and Mount Mary Church. Religion, I thought, was a surmountable obstacle in our marriage. So I sat before the havankund, as it blazed, revelling in the novelty of it all. The mantras being chanted by the priest, who very kindly translated each line he said into Hindi for my benefit, the kanyadaan or the giving away done by my husband's maternal uncle and his wife, because my mother was a widow, and therefore not allowed to do so by ritual. The seven rounds around the holy fire, with the shlokas being chanted was almost a mystical experience. I had seen this happen a million times in Hindi films, but nothing could have prepared me for the sudden shift within me which seemed to be happening with every step I was taking. It was almost as if I was shedding the carapace of the Kiran of yore, and emerging a different person, a new-born wife. And then, once we did the seven rounds around the fire, the sudden mantle of dignity that subtly descended on me. I was no longer the girl who expected to be indulged and pampered by everyone around me, and have things go my way always. I was a wife. I was responsible now not only for myself, but also for my husband, and my new family, who were welcoming me with a lot of love into their fold. And the simple act of sitting next to my new husband and performing the havan together, learning the simple way of putting the offerings into the havan, holding it right, was to me an indicator of how much I had to learn about the new life I was embracing.

And embracing willingly.

Kiran Manral

All for Love

'Where are you?' Abha questioned Imran on her new iPhone, which Imran had just got for her on their first anniversary.

'At my parent's house,' said Imran, and abruptly cut the call. This was usual whenever he was with his parents. Though used to it, I was very angry this time because he was returning from a tour, he knew I had been waiting for him for the last two hours, and now he had gone to meet his parents from the airport. They didn't like me but that didn't mean he could hang up on me.

Our marriage was full of controversies, with the material to make a complete blockbuster Bollywood movie. A Muslim boy marrying a Hindu girl, and that too, a Brahmin! An only son with five sisters. There was college romance, elopement and threats from the two families.

I was so used to being called a 'bitch' that I finally just accepted it as my second name. After our marriage, my parents forgave us and accepted us but Imran's parents refused to accept me. In the last one year, I had tried to apologise and impress them in every way, but all in vain. His mother called me the 'home breaker' and 'son stealer'. After a point, I decided to keep a distance.

And now, his mother had started recommending a beautiful Muslim girl for Imran to remarry. I freaked at the whole idea. Imran knew of my insecurities; he knew how deeply I loved him and had left my entire family just for him. I would often wonder what would happen if he actually left me for another girl.

Ironically, it was I who had forced him to visit them every weekend and give them a share of his salary, and now I was being rewarded for my efforts with a rival! It was absolutely atrocious and my patience had given way.

Imran reached home while I was still agonising and took me in his warm arms. I simply melted and sobbed even louder than before. He quickly got me a glass of water. His soft, soothing hands touched mine. I felt much better. He had been aware of the trauma and anxiety I had been going through, the mention of the second girl in his life had torn me apart.

He finally spoke, 'I have told Ammi that if she didn't accept you the way you were and who you were, she would have to part with her son. It was my last meeting with her today.' It was like a balm poured on my wounds.

'I have also told her that I love you and that you are a part of me. If she wanted my happiness, then she would have to accept you. I have also given her an ultimatum; if any of her nonsense persisted, we would shift to Bangalore.'

My heart skipped a beat. I thought I knew Imran and had been frustrated that he was letting his mother give me grief. Sometimes, I had doubted his commitment.

His standing up for me was like filling me with a new ray of hope, making me feel energetic and strong. His words must have had the desired impact for his mother invited us for lunch that Sunday, and since then has been good to me.

Finally, I felt that I was truly his bride, with all sides happy about this marriage.

Arti Sonthalia

Coffee

'Hello, it's me. How you doing?'

'Oh, you? I'm great! You?'

'I'm great too. Game for coffee?'

'It's one o'clock at night!'

'Big deal! Don't tell me you have grown all old and boring.'

'No! It's just that it was my girl's birthday today and I came back real late. I also have to reach office by nine.'

'I'm getting married tomorrow.'

'Oh!'

'What does that mean?'

'You are getting married tomorrow and you want to meet me now?'

'You don't want to meet me?'

'Why do you want to meet me, *now*?'

'For old time's sake.'

'I'll pick you up in thirty minutes.'

'Cool!'

I looked at myself in the mirror. Was it right to meet my ex, with not even twenty-four hours left for my wedding? With almost every one asleep, I could quietly sneak out and no one would ever notice. But the angel in me asked quite judgmentally, 'Is it right?' The devil in me reasoned, 'Is it absolutely wrong?' The angel said, 'You tell me!' The devil advocated my case with a strong argument, 'Primarily it should not be a problem as they would just meet for coffee. Moreover, she had never met him in the last five years as they had parted on quite a sour note. She has no residual love for him what so ever!' The angel in me smiled and said, 'Your points are all taken but please tell me, if this idea is so good, why on earth are you advocating it, Mr Devil?'

It was at that moment when I realised who the real devil was — my curiosity. That morning, when I had been to the beauty parlour for my pedicure, I had got engaged in a conversation with a couple of other brides-to-be. One rather bubbly girl had said, 'You will either want to kiss him or you will want to slap him and never see his face.' 'Wouldn't I be able to remain neutral?' I asked her. 'Nope,' she replied in a confident know-it-all voice. 'What if I want to kiss him?' asked another girl, who too seemed quite alarmed by this thought. The bubbly one replied with a mischievous gleam, 'Then you will find a way to kiss him.' The other one asked, 'If I did that, it would be wrong, *na*?' Bubbly girl said, 'Yes! Of course. That is how married women get lured into adultery.' We were served coffee, and the conversation drifted to another topic. But this idea lingered on in me, like an itch that refuses to leave. And suddenly in the middle of the night I had to know. It would be wrong to lead my future husband on, if I was even the least prone to adultery — a thought that had earlier never plagued my mind.

Still, the idea of venturing out at night seemed thrilling, a thing that gives you an adrenalin rush. I didn't know the real reason behind my going out, but I knew the solution lay in meeting him. And I needed to look great! Thankfully, because of the extra special bridal spa and beauty treatments, I was glowing and didn't need to worry about a zit or about how bad I might be looking. Even without make-up, I was glowing! I couldn't help being happy. A grand aunt who had come to stay with us for the wedding had said, 'Why go to the beauty parlour and spend so much? You're the bride, before marriage you would be naturally glowing.' I had brushed aside her theory. However, seeing my reflection in the mirror that night I questioned myself: Was it the treatments or was it merely a bride's blush? I blushed at the thought. Even though many people were referring to me as the bride constantly, and the rituals were supposed to accustom me to this idea, neither had I referred to myself as the bride, nor had I felt like one. Till now, that is.

I realised my name, my identity, my entire existence would change in a few more hours, it would all be attached to that of another man. I would be attached to a man who would pledge in front of the entire world that he would take care of me. I suddenly felt fragile, like the glass bangles kept on my dresser. I was supposed to wear them the next morning. From where I looked, they glistened and twinkled, like a child's bright eager eyes, willing to know more and more and more... I realised that my actions tonight might break them and I couldn't let that happen.

It was exactly at that moment that I dialled his number again. I didn't want to meet him any more. He took the call after about fourteen rings, a wait I consider too long.

'Yeah… I'm driving.'

'Why do you talk while driving, it's not right, you know.'

'Who cares? It's night time and you can bribe your way out…'

'It's illegal.'

'Ms Runway Bride, you don't have the right to judge, ha!'

'What do you mean?'

'What do I mean? What do you mean by asking me to meet you so late at night, just before your wedding? I'm not judging you, lady!'

I disconnected the phone. I couldn't talk further. My intentions had been pure. But now I felt embarrassed and cheap. That wasn't how I had perceived it all. I don't know about my adrenalin, but my blood rushed up my veins. In that moment I realised that it was his creepy mindset that had freaked me out. It was his crudeness that repulsed me and made me run as far away from him as possible. Hurt and bleeding I had been alone, for a long time, till someone put a band-aid on the bruises, wiped my tears and brought me coffee. Was I about to do something to hurt that someone? Memories of the past haunted me, and in a moment I relived a vast section of my vulnerable adulthood. And I knew the man who I was in love with now would be the one I'd love forever. I then dialled another number. And I confessed.

'So, do you still want to marry me tomorrow?' I asked. My feet felt cold, even though they were under a blanket. I waited with bated breath to hear him speak. Then after a moment's quiet, he spoke, 'Well, when I thought of marrying you, I knew you were a bit stupid. But now that I know *how* stupid you can be, I must protect you. Else this big bad world of wolves will eat this honest little girl up! Would you now care for some coffee, to battle your wedding jitters?' I laughed and cried, till the tears of my laughter mingled with those of sorrow and guilt, as I mumbled a yes. I knew the next day we would be quite a bleary eyed couple, in the photographs, but I also knew that we'd be one very much in love.

Joie Bose

Dowry Dilemma

As my wedding day drew near, I found myself in a dilemma. I was in love with my fiancé and was looking forward to spending the rest of my life with him. The issue was dowry, the ghost that haunts most Indian weddings, especially arranged ones.

There were no demands for dowry from my fiancé's family, but we belonged to the 'Vaish' or business community, and there was always an expectation of a certain scale of grandeur. My parents assured me repeatedly that it was well within their means.

I was the eldest of three sisters and had frequently heard relatives sympathising with my parents for having to marry off three daughters, with no sons to earn for them in their old age. And then there were horror stories about husbands and in-laws who kept a low profile at the time of the wedding, but later extorted money from the bride's parents for the rest of their lives! A distant relative, who knew both families, claimed that my future in-laws had expectations of a staggering amount of cash. The atmosphere at home was tense and I felt stifled.

Whenever I went out on a date with Rajesh, I would try to gauge his thoughts about dowry. His responses were always reassuring, but casual. My anxiety continued. My mother sensed my nervousness. 'Rajesh is a gem, and his family members are good people,' she comforted me.

As a bride, I looked perfect. The festive colour of my mehndi, my gorgeous pink tissue lehnga and the flowers in my elaborate hairdo, everything was wonderful but my worry had got the better of me.

The wedding ceremony had begun. Rajesh and I were sitting cross-legged in the mandap as the priests chanted the mantras and explained the significance of each ritual. I had a lump in my throat as it was time for the formal dahej or dowry procedure. My father was asked to give me a token sum of money that represented the entire dowry, which I dutifully passed to Rajesh. The priest then asked Rajesh to do what he thought was right, with the money. In keeping with the tradition, Rajesh had to pass it to his parents but instead, he passed it right back to me! Everyone around us broke into laughter. Tears streamed down my cheeks as my in-laws assured my parents that they wanted nothing more than their precious daughter from them.

In the past thirteen years, our marriage has had its share of ups and downs which I have been able to sail through armed with the certainty that I am, indeed, married to 'a gem of a person'!

Parul Gupta

Fairytale Bride

This incident took place a few years ago in Mumbai. My sister-in-law was getting married and around 150 of us had travelled from Ahmedabad to Mumbai by train to attend the nuptial rites. We had all stayed up the night singing, eating and dancing and looking forward to the upcoming festivities.

Upon arriving, we immediately got ready for the 'mehendi' ceremony, the atmosphere so thickly laden with gaiety that no one wanted to miss out on anything, so there was no question of resting!

I helped my sister-in-law dress for the function as part of the wedding duties allotted to me though there were professionals to take care of it. She, on the other hand, couldn't care less, so enraptured by the thought of getting married was she. Not that I blamed her, she and Ritesh (her fiancé) had had to wait an entire year before an auspicious date was chosen.

By about four o'clock, I was a bit worn out and wanted to retire to my room for a while but Shuchi, my sister-in-law, had other plans. She wanted to meet Ritesh and couldn't go un-chaperoned so I had to tag along with them. A little, no actually a lot weary of the unflagging energy of the bride, I tried to convince her otherwise, but my words fell on deaf ears. I resignedly went for a cup of coffee (which gave me constipation) and my eyes drooped despite their fervent chatter. Thankfully, we had to go back soon to get ready for the next function, which was on the terrace of the Leela Hotel. I managed to squeeze in a five-minute snooze before I got ready to escort a radiant Shuchi to the lobby where her younger brother-in-law took over to drive her to the venue.

The terrace was beautifully done up with diyas and flowers. The children had set up the stage for a small performance to welcome the bride-to-be. The celebrations were on full swing when suddenly there was a commotion on one side of the terrace. People ran with alarmed expressions, leaving us perplexed and none the wiser. Suddenly my husband grabbed Shuchi and me and made a beeline for the elevators. We were constantly asking him why we had to leave so abruptly, but he pushed us squarely into the car, mumbling almost as if to himself. A little confounded at this tomfoolery, Shuchi voiced her anger but was shut up by a single look from her brother.

We entered our suite, with not a single person in sight. Though puzzled, tiredness got the better of us and we dozed off.

Woken by some sounds, I glanced towards Shuchi who was deep in sleep, looking beautiful. A feeling of foreboding gripped me as I made my way to the lobby. I stopped in my tracks. The whole family gathered outside was looking devastated and deep in debate. I wondered what this Hitchcockian drama would reveal. Later, I got to know the point of altercation was breaking the news to Shuchi and who would do it.

Ritesh's younger brother had suffered a stroke when he had gone to the lavatory. The elders had considered it unwise to break the news at the venue so everyone had been called back to the hotel. Needless to say, the wedding would not take place and everyone's concern at that time was how Shuchi would react and how difficult it would be to pacify her. So engrossed in our discussion were we that no one noticed a white-faced Shuchi standing at the doorway.

As if sensing her presence suddenly, everyone looked in her direction, a haunted expression in her eyes. She must be crushed as there was nothing she had looked forward to with as much excitement as tying the knot with the man she loved.

She moved towards us, automaton-like, and just when I thought she was about to break down, she gave each of us a shock which we will remember forever. 'It's a shame that you people, who are my family, think I am so fragile that all you can think of is how will I be able to bear this unkind act of God. What about the man I love? Hasn't he just lost his brother? What about his mother who lost a twenty-two-year-old son? At a time like this, our thoughts and prayers should be with them to give them strength to endure the catastrophe that has fallen on them so suddenly.'

The gravity of what she said hit us like a ton of bricks... We always underestimated the fortitude of a woman in love.

In the coming months, life hobbled on and Shuchi tried to help Ritesh and his bereaved family, but the thought that she would be held indirectly responsible as it had happened on the eve of her entering their family didn't look like a good omen.

One day, out of the blue, Ritesh's family came over to our place and we were ecstatic when they said they wanted to set a wedding date. Everyone looked overjoyed but for Shuchi, who glanced nervously at her mother-in-law. And as if she read her mind and understood her quandary, she smiled reassuringly at Shuchi and nodded her head.

We were back in Mumbai. This time much less in number but high in spirit, everyone who had indulged the bride earlier looked at her with new-found respect. The ceremony straight out of a story book with the enamoured groom and vestal bride, enthralling the people who had come to bless the couple, hoping this time they took home a flavour of cheer.

Shashi Agarwal

I Do

When you look at me I look away,
When I grin you smile.
When I hop on the pavement,
with care, you make way,
with a look which says you would walk, with me, like this
for miles…

Those reassuring words
straight from the heart,
That beautiful light of forever-ness
straight from the start.

That dent on the right,
leaves me wounded.
That innocent smile,
renders me daunted.

Those little bouts of anger
that you happily endure.

Those mood swings you heartily accept
which can, and do, injure...

For all the reasons you make me smile,
For all the reasons my life is on a new high.
For all your promises, come what may, you would never bid
Adieu
I proudly declared to the world,

'I do.'

Mariya Salim

Opposites Attract

It was only when two old friends decided to get married that the differences in the families became apparent. My family had been partying and his were following all the much anticipated rituals in honour of the son getting finally married.

My mehndi ceremony was a complete riot with my brothers practicing their moves to lift me up as a surprise during the mala badal. His family had the traditional simanth puja.

I walked into the wedding hall in my wedding paraphernalia, to be told to hustle to the dressing room at the back as I was not to be seen. Ok, I had my cronies with me, and the giggles continued till we realised the 'boy's side' was merely on the other side of the partition.

My in-the-making husband kept telling me to look down/ act demure/ don't show all your teeth as we were going through the rituals. All I could hear were the brothers guffawing while they joked about what they were planning, and laughing with them as they warned me to 'do it first'! Slam, dunk! They lifted me up perfectly as I placed the mala around my husband, first! And to this day I regret not carrying a camera along with a

mala as, much to his horror, the groom found his demure bride
lifted beyond his reach. Quick thinking friends lifted him up
too, and he placed his mala around me in traditional Bengali
style, much, much to the bemusement of his side of the guests.

I had put my foot down about the raja-rani chairs for us in
the dais. But the rest of the reception was a typical affair, with
bright halogens and the photographer taking group pictures of
everyone queuing to give the bride and groom their blessings
and casseroles and sundry other utensils. Little did the boy's
family know about the fully equipped car in the parking lot,
complete with ice, glasses and assorted goodies. Our friends
weren't about to be cheated out of the merriment. I do think
my dad did partake too, and I have never seen my mum move
as fast as she did when someone handed me an innocuous
glass of coke, at least the mother of the bride had to ensure she
doesn't get anything she shouldn't.

Ten years later, we had an anniversary party. Good friends,
good food, good music, good drinks and some great dance
moves. Very sweetly, my sisters-in-law offered to get us malas
for the function we were calling a party. By the time they
realised I was serious about the no mala bit, up came another
bone of contention. I insisted the kids in the family (friends'
children were not invited, however close we are) be sent home
after dinner. There was much opposition ranging from 'your
niece wants to be there for your function' to 'my daughter may
not want to leave without me'. My own children were looking
forward to their pajama party, dark room hide-and-seek and
jelly and ice cream with their cousins and didn't understand
the opposition. The kids had a blast, and I completely enjoyed
my sisters-in-law dancing in child-free abandonment.

Yes, the families are very different. But their whole hearted acceptance of the differences and their affection despite the differences is what is more important. The main ingredient to keeping us all together. For ever.

Monisha Sen

Slow Down ... Please!

A 'wedding-house' in India is like a base camp for the battlefield. Numerous arrangements have to be made, right from booking the hotel, fixing the menu to distributing cards and gifts; and so much more. I had the luxury to not be a part of the 'planning committee'. An 'army' of uncles, aunts, cousin brothers and sisters meticulously worked towards achieving perfection in organising everything.

Everybody teased me by saying that I should enjoy my last few days as a bachelor, by living the way I wanted to, because once I got married, it would all change. I was into Sales and thus conditioned to be aggressive, chasing targets and rushing after deadlines. I liked to live my life on the fast track and that is how I intended it to be, no matter what anybody said.

The 'D-Day' arrived and the religious ceremony at the Gurudwara started. We had to take four pheras around the Guru Granth Sahib ji — the holy scripture of Sikhism. A palla (cloth) is held by the bride which the groom keeps on his shoulder and leads the way. As soon as the priest asked me to begin the pheras, I got up and started walking at a rapid pace.

I was halfway when the priest signalled and said, 'Slow down, slow down please.' As I turned around, I noticed my lovely bride Preeti looking flustered. She was having a tough time keeping up with me in her heavy bridal finery. As I looked at her, she did not say anything but her eyes spoke volumes. I altered my pace, taking care of Preeti's comfort, and completed the pheras.

My relatives laughed at this, but I realised my life had truly changed forever. It was no longer just 'me', but 'we' who now had to walk this journey of life at a pace which is 'just right' for both of us!

Vijayendra Haryal

The Blushing Groom

It's the 30th of August, and as I dress mechanically, I keep my fingers crossed and pray that the outcome is different from the earlier time.

It starts raining as I drive to the temple. It doesn't seem like a harbinger of good tidings in this dismal atmosphere. I try and look upbeat as I spot Deepak talking to the pundit, but his wry smile tells me my efforts are in vain. He looks at his watch nervously as the pundit explains to me the importance of the ritual (kanyadaan) that I am going to perform at the behest of Deepak, who has grown as dear as Sanchita, my best friend and his future wife. The same question is on everyone's mind as they are part of the scene they have witnessed before, 'Will she come?'

Sanchita and Deepak were college friends but drifted apart when both got married to their respective sweethearts. Secretly, Sanchita always had a crush on Deepak but apart from her closest friends, no one knew about it. She married, however, her best friend in college, Sandeep, much against her father's wishes, but soon realised that a good friend may not necessarily make a good husband too. During one of her low phases, she bumped into Deepak, and before no time, they revived their old friendship and she found a shoulder to cry on. Sandeep of course knew about her crush on Deepak during their college days and would never tolerate it, so she kept it a secret from him. Soon Deepak, who had been divorced shortly after he had gotten married, confessed that he was in love with Sanchita and even though she loved him equally, she had two children so she was resigned to the fate of a cheerless marriage with Sandeep. Deepak was ready to do literally anything for her — marriage or a live-in relationship or an affair, whatever she wanted.

Sanchita did not have the guts to ask Sandeep for a divorce, so once, in her desperation, she agreed to run away with Deepak. He booked flight tickets to go to his sister who stayed abroad. Sanchita had packed a bag with clothes for herself and her younger daughter who she planned to take with her, and given it to Deepak days in advance. That day she had to attend a family wedding and she had calculated that since everyone would be busy, no one would miss her. Deepak's friend was to pick her up at 9 p.m. and take her to Baroda from where she and Deepak would fly off to their new home. At quarter-to-nine, she touched her father's feet for his blessings and quickly left the marriage hall. Throughout the drive, she was uneasy and the best efforts of her escort wouldn't put her at ease. Suddenly when they had covered most of the distance, she told him to drop her off, and that she couldn't go any further. There were no mobile phones but somehow he got her to talk to Deepak but she wouldn't change her mind. Deepak flew alone and stayed there for a month.

Another time she was going to the US with her parents, so he too flew there and they decided to run away, but this time too, luck was not in their favour as her mother was diagnosed with cancer and she didn't have the heart to leave her side.

In the meantime, her marriage went from bad to worse and she got a divorce. Now finally we thought she and Deepak would be married, but we were wrong. She didn't want to give custody of her children to Sandeep, and they would never accept Deepak as their father.

She went through a lot of hardships at that time, common friends stopped inviting her, so loneliness was a big part of her life, not to mention financial problems. She even started designing clothes for friends to earn extra money. Running the house alone and single-handedly bringing up two children was taking its toll. I, for one, wondered how much more Deepak would wait for her as he already had for ten years, but to my surprise, he wasn't ready to give up yet. Finally, one day she agreed to get married and we quickly set the earliest date possible.

On the appointed day, I was to pick up Sanchita and take her to the temple where she and Deepak were to get married. When I reached her place, she wasn't there, I couldn't contact her, and I just assumed that she had left without me as I was late by a few minutes. When I reached the temple, she hadn't reached and obviously that made me doubt whether she would come at all and sure enough she didn't. I remember the resigned look on Deepak's face and when I asked him if we should go find her, he refused and turned away quietly.

When I went back to Sanchita's, all my anger towards her vapourised. Her eyes were swollen from weeping and as soon as she saw me, she hugged me and broke down. She said she had visited her lawyer that morning and he had told her that she might lose custody of her children if she remarried. I wanted to ask her a lot of things but refrained as this was not the time.

Deepak withdrew into a shell, he wouldn't take any calls from anyone and through some friends, we got to know he had gone away to live with his sister. All Sanchita's efforts to get in touch with him proved futile. She was overwrought and became reclusive. At times when she was distracted, she vented all her frustration on her children.

Then one day, she read an obituary in the newspaper. Deepak's uncle had passed away so she called me up and we went there to offer our condolences. We encountered a very nonplussed Deepak at the entrance. For a minute he looked awkward, but the moment he saw her moist eyes, he hugged her and held her close. There was a lump in my throat and I could see Deepak trying hard to control his emotions.

That evening, when Sanchita went home, she noticed a feeling of tranquility and completeness after a long time. Suddenly it struck her that she had left Deepak for her children and in the bargain they all had been miserable but if she was happy she would be a much better mother too. She knew now her happiness lay with Deepak and she had taken his love for granted. She would fight for the custody of her children but for now she knew what she had to do. This time the bride-to-be must shed her baggage of responsibilities.

Just ten minutes left and I can see the sweat beads on Deepak's brow, his sister in a state of near panic, when a car drives up and all eyes turn expectantly and one can hear the collective sigh of relief when Sanchita steps down from the car followed by both her daughters. I glance towards Deepak, his face beaming, and I must add this is the first time that the groom is blushing more than the bride.

Shashi Agarwal

The Saint

My dearest friend Smita and her beau Siddarth were seeing each other for over three years. So, they wanted to settle down as soon as possible. But there was a hitch. Siddarth's elder brother Soham was yet to be married — the main cause for his parents to delay their second son's marriage too.

The two brothers were like best of friends; Soham had his own plans — to go abroad, earn a fortune and other things he'd never told anyone. So, when he got to know that both were tired of waiting, he told Sid (as we call him) to go ahead.

Soham, who was more like a friend to all of us, went ahead and told his mom that she shouldn't wait for him. She got furious. But she had no alternative. She knew both her sons were as strong-willed as she was. Once a thing is decided, it is decided, no going back on it. Toeing that line, once Sid had decided that he would marry Smita only, he wouldn't go back on his word. The mother did her best to convince her sons to marry girls of her choice, but they wouldn't relent.

One day, just before they decided to go for the first lot of shopping for Sid's family, his mother felt restless. Smita asked

her, 'What happened. Why are you so worried?' Almost on
the verge of tears, the mother said, 'How I wished Soham had
married first...' Smita immediately rang me up and told me
how her mom-in-law was crying. I felt for the mother and
suggested, 'Would you like to take her to a religious scholar and
saint who finds solutions through prayers to solve problems?'

I knew this gentleman from Haridwar who lived in a small
house in South Delhi. He is a quiet social worker and would
never take anything in return for his services.

Smita suggested it to Sid's mom and she jumped at the
suggestion. 'Why not? Can we go today? Right now?' she
asked. For her, every moment counted.

Well, I introduced Sid, Smita and her to-be-parents-in-law
to Babaji without revealing their relationship. As he saw Sid,
he said, 'Who is this boy, his face is radiating with grace. He
is a good boy.' I could see Smita smiling with pride. For her, it
was like an approval from a seer. She felt comfortable about
her choice. Then I revealed their relationship and told him that
Sid's mother had come for his blessings as well as for help to
solve her problems.

The scholar ran his experienced eyes over her and told her
to ask whatever she wanted to openly. Before she spoke, she
looked at me pointedly. I understood she didn't want to reveal
her family secrets in front of me. I suggested that I would go
out. Sid, Smita and Soham too got up with me saying, 'You be
comfortable, Ma. We will come back when you are through.'

We returned after almost an hour. All smiles, Sid's mother
took him to a secluded corner and said, 'Everything will be
okay now, I hope. He has told me some prayers which will be
very effective to solve the problems.' I couldn't hear the rest

as she started whispering. Smita was standing next to me. She didn't seem to mind the mother and son's private talks.

But what followed took my breath away. I saw Sid shouting at his mother and trying to escape from her clutches. He blurted, 'This is what you had actually come here for? That's why I didn't want to bring you here ... I knew it, I knew it...' and he walked away. I couldn't understand anything. Smita rushed to Sid and asked, 'What happened? You can't behave with her like that in the middle of the road!'

Sid stopped and gave her a sad look. He looked helpless, pained and distressed. A shiver ran through me. By then his mother had also come up. Without looking at me, she sat in the car.

As they dropped me home, I invited all of them over to have a cup of tea. The parents refused, but I insisted. As I was preparing tea for them, Sid and Smita joined me. All of a sudden, Sid put his hand around Smita's shoulder firmly and said, 'Let mom go to any saint or baba and try to find remedies to break our alliance. I will never cheat you. I have told her, if I don't marry you, I won't marry at all. I won't marry a girl of her choice for sure. Not because I have a problem with her choice, but because I love you and have already promised that I would marry you...'

I nearly dropped the cup I was holding. Tears rolled down Smita's eyes as she saw his parents busy talking to my parents over snacks. Sid's mother had used my connection to sabotage my best friend's own life — her bahu-to-be! Going to find a solution for Soham had just been an excuse to hide her real intentions!

Sid, of course, kept his word and they married soon after amid a seemingly happy atmosphere. Smita looked resplendent in her bridal finery and I think it had to do more with the love that she saw in her husband's eyes than all the make-up and hair styling!

Today Smita has forgiven Sid's possessive mother who, like any other typical Indian mother, thinks that only she can take right decisions for her son.

It's been almost a decade since their marriage and each time I see them together with their two cute little kids, I see in Sid a man who stood by my best pal, despite all the objections from none other than his own loving mother. And needless to say, Smita still considers it as her most treasured memory from her married life.

Rana Siddiqui Zaman

To Be with the One You Love

From planning trips to planning dinners out to planning weekends, my life at every stage has been planned. And I like to plan ahead of the actual event. So, it is but natural that when my boyfriend proposed to me in August 2007, I started my research and planning for my wedding though I knew it was at least a year away.

I read articles in *Cosmo* about the best wedding locales in India. Kerala and Goa emerged with many, many options but when I discussed it with Amma, she said it didn't make sense. We would have to make arrangements for everyone attending the wedding and our 'everyone' is a large number. That is when I first realised that my wedding was not going to be my ideal wedding.

What is my ideal wedding? Well, I always wanted a temple wedding in a heritage temple like the ones in Bellur and Hallebidu. I had seen these temples when I was ten, and though I deny dreaming about and planning my wedding since then, I think somewhere deep down I saw myself being married there. I always wanted a traditional wedding with a small number of people — just the close ones who mattered to me and for whom my wedding was a priority, not just curiosity.

Going ahead with my planning to cut down the travel and the trouble people who come from outside Bengaluru would have to take, I then decided that I would find a place that resembles the picture of my ideal wedding. So the hunt began for a quaint, traditional venue within Bengaluru. Sadly, with that filter, I was left with two options: Villa Potipatti in Malleshwaram and Ganjam Mantapa in Basavangudi.

Ganjam Mantapa was near where we stay and hence worked for everyone. But for me it worked because it was the closest option I had to my dream location. This mantap is a beautiful ancestral home, with a tiled roof, red oxide flooring, wooden railing for the spiral staircase and plenty of natural light. This was unlike the other halls in the city which translate grand to chandeliers, red carpets, weird paintings and all things that according to me are just gaudy.

So in April 2008, when the wedding dates were fixed, the first thing I did was call Ganjam Mantapa (yes, I already had their number) and book the mantap. This was the highest priority on my wish list.

Once I got Ganjam Mantapa, I was willing to listen to things related to what I had to wear, the number of poojas, the number of events and the guests. All of it was worth it, as Ganjam Mantapa made my wedding as close to ideal as possible in Bengaluru.

My fiancé loved the place too. In fact, we had already made a trip there in January 2008 and were delighted at the thought of getting married in such a quaint home. Something about it being an ancestral home added so much to our wedding.

One thing I had not accounted for was that once the parents and families get involved, your wedding planning becomes more of a nightmare. My parents are very social people and I have liked that about them. So as they worked on the guest list, 200 guests became 250 and then 300. Slowly, I was pushing my friends into different events to keep the guest list within 400, which was Ganjam Mantapa's people capacity.

The truth that this wedding is ours not yours, just yours to give us is something parents fail to understand. It is always their wedding for them with their kids in it planning things the way they want.

Finally, one fine day, my parents decided to change the venue to accommodate the increasing guests. It hurt me terribly that my parents did not want to hurt their acquaintances by not allowing them to participate in our wedding but yet, they were completely willing to consciously bypass our wishes and carry on with their changed agendas expecting us to go along with enthusiasm as they love us and always want the best for us.

My parents hunted for an alternate location, visiting many halls with a larger capacity. I was upset that we were no longer saying our vows at Ganjam Mantapa. The thought of getting married in a red carpeted, bulb-filled, white walled, air-conditioned hall in front of 200 friends and 400 strangers made me very sad.

I remember my fiancé and I tried to see if we could make our parents change their decisions, and finally, after failing, we just consoled each other. And it is when he was consoling me that he said the sweetest thing, 'I really like Ganjam Mantapa... I like it even more because you like it.'

Those words just made me fall in love with him all over again. He gave me hope — hope that he will stand by me and will never intentionally hurt my feelings or disregard my wishes. And if he ever did, I guess he will at least know the right things to say. So though my wedding preparation was not going as planned, I was glad it was with the man I love because well, even that could have been changed! I realised then that this may be a small sacrifice I would have to make to be with the one I love.

Where did we finally get married, you ask? Well, it was at Ganjam Mantapa! With every visit to the large wedding halls my parents realised why I had insisted on Ganjam Mantapa. They saw that more the flamboyance, lesser the warmth of the hall. So on the 21st of December, 2008, we tied the knot in the ancestral home of the Ganjam Jewellers amongst close friends and family. Despite all the drama around the wedding, I would love to go through it all over again.

Vibha Karnik

We Are Married and We Still Date

I just came across a heading that read 'We don't date, we just marry', and believe me, since the time I read it, I have been trying to extract the real meaning out of it. My heart and brain had a few contradictions and, as in my case, I felt a more appropriate header would be 'We are married and we still date'.

I say this as I am all set to celebrate my third marriage anniversary with my sweet and loving hubby, Varun, on the 20th of April. Three years. The time sounds so long but has really passed like a blink of an eye and most of my friends who are married for a longer period would second me on this.

As I sit here in front of my laptop, penning down my thoughts, I still feel those goose bumps which I had, while preparing for the D-Day. My entire house was occupied with friends and relatives and suggestions were pouring in from all sides. The excitement of getting married to the person whom I loved came hand-in-hand with a feeling of heaviness in the heart for having to leave my mom, sis, grandparents and my home. It was certainly a difficult moment.

Year one was a new experience as it came like a surprise. Though we had known each other for a long time, it made us realise how unknown we were to each other. The food he liked, the songs I loved, his favourite shirt, my best actor.... Oh my God, the list was too long and it was fun to get to know each other. The entire year was exciting and enjoyable.

Year 2007, i.e. the second year, brought many expectations with it. The concentration was now more on making a home out of a house. We thought more about our future and ways to improve it. And we really made the old saying true: 'A wife and husband are like the two wheels of a vehicle, and coordination between them is a must.'

The wheels moved together at a good pace and we stepped into the third year of our marriage... It was a year of exchange of souls... (Not trying to sound like Paulo Coelho). The year actually brought a transformation in our lives. Our dialogues changed... He spoke my words and I spoke his... Our likes and interests exchanged... Sometimes we laughed at ourselves... And gradually we reached a more mature stage... Even our silence was meaningful and we understood each other better than ever.

Today, as I write this journal, I feel satisfied as these words echo in my mind: 'A successful marriage requires falling in love many times, and always with the same person.' I would certainly love to fall in love again and again, for many years to come, with my wonderful husband.

Rediscovering each other is the only way to be married and still be dating!

Hema Dhawan

Wedding Blues

More than three decades ago, in a land not far away, there was a small town girl and a big city boy who fell in love and decided to get married. Their parents had known each other for eons, so the match was approved (with mutual sighs of relief) and the D-Day decided. The girl had cleared her IAS written exams and had bartered what may have been a civil servant's job for sacred marriage vows. The boy, a conscientious and dutiful soul, was completely aware of the financial burden a happy ceremony like marriage dragged with it. Thus, magnanimously, he distributed clothes to all and sundry who were to attend the wedding from his side, threatening them not to make any demands on his beloved's family.

But a problem arose in the guise of the girl's mother. A traditional, headstrong lady who had wed her elder daughter off with the pomp and grandeur a wedding demanded, insisted her younger daughter meet then same fate. So, with a will to win, she pursued her son-in-law to find out what was it that she could gift him. Most of the times he avoided her, but when confronted, he'd cheekily answer 'an underwear' or 'a hat' (remember she had seen him since he was a baby, so such liberties were permissible). Finally, realising that the guy was determined not to receive any item that could even remotely be termed as dowry, she decided to tackle the problem secretly.

In the not-yet-so-hot month of March, dressed in her red and gold finery, the girl sat beside the suited boy, the sacred fire dancing in front of them to the chants of the prayers. The girl's mother sat, with a hawk's eye on the proceedings, and waited for the cue. At the pre-decided moment, she placed before her few-minutes-left-to-be son-in-law a nine-diamond ring. The girl looked away. She knew of her mother's plan and had been unable to alter her mind. The guy looked flummoxed. It was unexpected. His hand formed a fist and he refused to touch the ring, leave alone try it for size.

The girl's mom was now raging. She asked the priest to stop chanting. The ceremony would not proceed unless the guy accepted the ring. Guests looked quizzical, perhaps wondering if dinner would be served even if the marriage was cancelled! At last the girl's sensible, peace-loving father intervened. He cajoled the guy to accept the gift, whispering that they'd discuss the issue later. The guy was embarrassed into relenting. The priest resumed chanting, the guests stroked their empty bellies and the girl's mother smiled smugly. The boy wasn't so hopeless after all!

Now, after thirty three years of togetherness, the ring remains in the same box in the couple's cupboard. The diamonds still glitter. The ring may not be new but it is still unworn. The couple laugh when they recount the incident. Age has softened the girl's mother. She laughs with them too. But the fate of the ring has been decided. It will be presented to the couple's son-in-law whenever their wayward daughter decides to marry.

And I hope my husband and I will be able to pass it on, again unused, to another generation of men who value their women more than they love their gold.

Richa Wahi

2

POPPING THE QUESTION

When you realize you want to spend the rest of your life with somebody, you want the rest of your life to start as soon as possible.

—When Harry Met Sally

Popping the Question

Down on one knee, he put forth his hand. She smiled down sweetly, and linked hands with him. 'Will you marry me?' he whispered, his eyes shadowed with nervousness. 'Yes! A thousand times, yes,' she said ecstatically, before pulling him up for an embrace.

As the schmaltzy music reached a crescendo, I turned my eyes off the TV screen to glare at the man plonked beside me on the sofa.

'You never proposed to me,' I accused.

He looked confused. 'What...' he began.

'P-r-o-p-o-s-e,' I enunciated. 'You never asked me to marry you,' I added for good measure, wanting to set things straight right away.

'But we're married,' said the man.

'I know that,' I retorted. 'But you never went down on a knee and asked me to marry you. You just asked when we would get married!'

My exasperated husband looked at me as if I was a brightly lit up Christmas tree on which the lights had suddenly blacked out.

I looked at him expectantly.

Brought up on a diet of Victorian-era classics followed by countless romantic novels, I, like many other women, believed in the inviolate sanctity of 'The Marriage Proposal'.

The excessively maudlin movie had made me realise that I had been short-changed.

Didn't men across the world do the weirdest, wildest things for their lady loves? Some penned love letters, others planned imaginative outings, a few got a cake iced and affixed a solitaire in the centre, some waited for the girlfriend to sip the glass of champagne till she reached the ring, while a few over-the-top proposers paid for planes to fly past with a banner asking the big Q.

Hell, even Mr Big went the 'ever thine, ever mine, ever ours' way when he finally popped the question to *Sex and the City*'s Carrie Bradshaw.

I looked at him, a question in my eyes.

'We didn't need a marriage proposal,' he said.

My eyes widened; the question in them grew bigger.

'A marriage proposal is necessary for those not sure of the other. Where there is a question of "yes" or "no",' he said. 'But we, we're complementary. We're yin and yang, spice and sugar, cheese and wine, basically two halves of a whole. There was only one way this relationship was heading. Marriage. I knew that as well as you did,' he added. 'Why else did I ask when we were getting married?'

I was flabbergasted. And the smile was back on my face again.

Teja Lele

Reluctant Bride, Adamant Bridegroom

Umar was in a dilemma. He loved Shirin, of course, and wanted very much to marry her. Not just that, Ammi had had the most beautiful silk garara stitched and decorated with silver and gold sequins and had bought a glittering though delicate diamond studded ring for the bride-to-be. And that wasn't all. Just last night the entire khandaan had attended the manjha ceremony at his house and he had posed with every known cousin, uncle and aunt, looking every inch the happy and expectant bridegroom.

The trouble was… Shirin didn't want to marry him!

'Don't get me wrong,' she had explained over an ISD call, 'You're a wonderful person. I've known you all my life and I know any girl will be lucky to be your wife.'

'Then what's your problem… What'll I say to Ammi? She's made me go through all the haldi and mehndi and manjha rituals, determined that you'll be her bahu.'

'The problem, dear man, is that I have no intentions of leaving Lucknow and settling in far away Karachi.'

'C'mon Shiri, Karachi is closer to Lucknow than Mumbai is.'

'You know very well what I mean, Um. Timbuctoo may be a hundred times the distance from here than your city is, but it's easier to go there. I'll be stuck across the border what with the erratic way in which your government behaves in matters of diplomacy.'

'Leave the politics out, will you. You'll be marrying me, not the Secretary of Foreign Affairs.'

'Um, that's not funny and don't make it hard for me, please.' A hint of tears and then, 'Just tell Khalajaan, Shiri said NO.'

I wish it was that easy, Umar sighed. Shiri was his cousin. Their mothers were sisters. Unfortunately, they lived on opposite sides of the LOC and now that was posing a big hurdle in the way of his happiness.

Ammi wasn't one to take defeat easily. Don't take 'no' for an answer, she had told him categorically. When you land in Lucknow with the nikah ka joda, she'll have to concede. Once Ammi had decided upon bringing her niece, her beloved and only sister's pretty though a trifle headstrong daughter home as a bride for her youngest son, no one could make her budge from her decision!

Next time Um called Shiri, Ammi grabbed the phone from his hand…

'Hey *ladki! Kyun adanga laga rahi hai shaadi mein*? Your parents are agreeable, your grandparents want nothing more than for our families to have a new tie, we're SO fond of you and poor Umar is dying a thousand deaths with every phone call of yours. Now be sensible and come right back here with him and that's final!' she screamed into the receiver.

If anyone had to hear this strange conversation between Ammi and her prospective daughter-in-law, one would be certain both were mad.

The next day he boarded the flight for India. None of his siblings had agreed to accompany him. How funny we'll look returning without the bride. We'll cut a sorry figure and be the laughing stock of the whole family. No baba, you go alone and do your best. Our wishes go with you. Only Ammi still firmly believed that Umar and Shirin would really tie the knot!

Now he had landed in Lucknow with a bag carrying the shimmering garara and the ring sitting pretty in its tiny velvet box.

Shirin was there to receive him. One look at the tall, handsome, young man with sleek though tousled hair and laughing eyes made her heart flutter... But no, she mustn't stumble from her resolve. Um was the best in the world but she couldn't allow herself to be uprooted from the safe comfort of her homeland. Nevertheless, she gave him a warm hug and a beaming smile.

'Welcome Um.'

Shirin's parents, grandparents, aunts and uncles had all greeted him with hugs and handshakes and inquired in whispers... 'You're here, does that mean she said "yes" to you?'

But when he tried to hand over the shagun to the ladies of the house, they wouldn't touch the bag. It can't be accepted unless the girl is willing, they explained sadly. So, the joda found a place in an empty shelf of a wall closet and there it would stay until the time Um was able to convince Shiri that Pakistan wasn't such a jungle of savages and hooligans as she imagined.

That night, Nanajan, Nani, Khalu and Khalajan summoned Um. She's being foolish, and immature. The loss will be hers entirely if she turns down your proposal, not to mention the embarrassment it'll bring to all of us. We have used every tactic with her. Still, we can't compel her to say yes. Now it's up to you.

Um stood up with a sudden determination.

'Can I take her out for dinner, please?'

'Of course, Beta.'

The whole family waited impatiently for their return. At last the bell rang and when the door opened, the entire family crowded at the entrance, looking expectantly at Um.

'Shiri says "yes". She's accepted my proposal.'

Silence! Then all eyes turned to Shirin. A rosy blush had spread over her pretty face and their Ms Down-to-Earth actually had a coy look about her!

'How did you achieve the impossible?' they chorused in unison.

Um winked at them boyishly...

'That's another story,' he said, glancing sideways at Shirin and everyone burst into happy and relieved laughter.

After the nikah, the family closed in on Umar again.

'Tell us what made her change her mind.'

Umar laughed.

'I trapped her. First I told her that I had no intentions of leaving India without taking her with me as my bride and if she didn't concede and I overstayed my visa, everyone would be in big trouble. That actually frightened her. Then I told her perhaps I wouldn't come back a second time for her. That did the trick, she agreed fast enough.'

(This is the story of one of the sweetest couples I know. Shirin is doing extremely well for herself in Karachi. Shirin and Umar have a lovely daughter, now almost eighteen. They visit Lucknow every year.)

Rehana Ali

The Perfect Match

'Marriage is not a ritual or an end. It is a long, intricate and intimate dance together and nothing matters more than your own sense of balance and your choice of partner.'

–Amy Bloom

As soon as I finished college, I could see tension build up on my parents' foreheads. After all, we did live in a nation obsessed with marriage at the 'right age' for girls.

My mother was no exception and was soon consumed with the objective of executing 'Operation Abhilasha Marriage'. I gave her my consent to search for a suitable bridegroom for me only to keep her busy for a while and save myself from the constant pestering. But one should never underestimate the efficiency of mothers. She instantly produced a thick file consisting of the profiles of prospective 'perfect husband material'. I was cornered.

It was a chunky file indeed. I needed help to make the right choice and the only person I could think of was Rajiv, my childhood friend. He was appointed as the 'Chief Selection Officer' as we sat down to scrutinise the profiles.

'Five foot ten inches, good-looking, only son. Interests — travelling, reading, music. How does this sound?' asked Rajiv.

'Very interesting. What's his name?' I enquired.

'Rajiv Agarwal, MBA and self employed,' he replied cheekily.

'That is your name and this is no joke,' I retorted.

In the next hour, we had short-listed two profiles. One should never underestimate the efficiency of fathers as well. A meeting was fixed with one of the boys for the very next day. I was impressed with all the groundwork that had been done. I asked Rajiv to come along with me because he knew me too well and I valued his opinion.

The boy arrived an hour late, which was a disappointing start. It was annoying and I was ready to leave, but Rajiv asked me to keep my cool and wait. After the meeting, Rajiv agreed with me when I expressed that he was far from impressive.

We met the second boy over lunch the next day. He was punctual, well dressed and created a good 'first impression'. Rajiv ordered a light meal for us at the coffee shop and we began our 'interview'. Within moments, it was obvious that the man had been forced by his parents to come and meet me. He was in love with another woman who they disapproved of. I heaved a sigh of relief as he was obviously ruled out.

As we drove home, I remarked, 'That is it. I guess it is just not meant to be for now.'

Rajiv pulled over the car, looked in my eyes and said, 'Well, you may not have found him yet, but I am very lucky to have found someone.'

'Who is she?' I was surprised and curious.

'You,' he said and held my hand.

I was stunned as our past flashed in front of my eyes. There had been moments when I was jealous seeing him with any other girl. There were times when I would miss him badly and had called him in the middle of the night. Had we moved beyond being 'just good friends'? I had been ignorant of my feelings for Rajiv which were obviously there because I was elated! We had grown up together, and had been the best of friends. Our families had been friends for years and we were happiest in each other's company.

'What are you thinking? It is perfectly alright if you don't feel the same way. I am your friend and would still help you find a suitable boy.'

I smiled and said nothing. For the first time, I was sure about what I wanted for the rest of my life. Rajiv knew the answer too. We drove home, silent and contented.

We have been married for fifteen years. Rajiv conceitedly claims that he knew it all along that I could never love anybody but him.

I really believe that I am fortunate to have someone whom I can truly call my soulmate, after all you don't find the perfect match in a pulled over vehicle every day!

Abhilasha Agarwal

The Proposal

At sixteen, I didn't know what falling in love meant, least of all, love at first sight. The hormones were raging and every time a girl smiled at me, it felt like love at first sight.

I was typically the good looking, fair, straight-nosed guy found in abundance in and around Delhi. After school, engineering college was a lot of fun and attraction to the fairer sex was spontaneous.

Four years whizzed past, at the end of which I was a certified electronics engineer — ready to dazzle the world with my knowledge and skill. I was lucky to get a good job while still in my final year. This was exhilarating as it meant financial independence.

My new job would take me to Bihar, and I was excited as I would finally get a chance to be the master of my own will. I bought a second-hand red motorbike. I also bought a pair of white driving gloves.

It was my first day and I drove my shiny new motorbike to report at my new office. As the day progressed, I found myself bored. All I could see was more and more guys and no girls! A couple of minutes later, three girls walked in. There was silence as the boys stared at them.

One of them was sitting quietly. Dressed in a brown sleeveless outfit with white polka dots, she had straight long hair pulled into a ponytail and twinkling black eyes. I think it was her eyes that first drew me to her. But then again, at my stage in life, everything caught my attention.

I smiled at her and we got chatting. I found out that she was the reading type while I was the outdoor type. Later, I tried to impress her by reading a couple of books and discussing them with her. We quickly became friends and started hanging out together.

The office had a welcome party for the freshers. I asked her to dance with me. That was the first time I touched her. It was electric. I was intrigued by her as she sang a few old Hindi film songs in a melodious voice. It was a magical evening and I was a little drunk and she looked radiant in a beautiful white dress with a pearl necklace.

Had I fallen in love? Was it for real this time? She was tall and good-looking, had a professional engineering degree, was modern and progressive, came from a good family and the best part was that she was cool and we got along well. After office hours, I missed being with her, talking and walking with her.

The vibes became stronger. The hours spent with her passed by too quickly and I started looking for excuses to be with her. Her mother made excellent pakoras and that was a good enough reason for me to visit her house almost every other day.

Finally, it was the last day of the induction and we all went out for a picnic. Walking along aimlessly, the two of us got separated from the group. We were on the gentle hill slopes of the Chhotnagpur plateau, amidst green surroundings. I picked up a piece of sugarcane and nervously began to chew on it. As I hummed a song, I looked into those twinkling black eyes, and blurted out, 'I love you and want to marry you!'

An awkward silence followed and I regretted taking her unawares. But she started laughing and pointed at my face. My front tooth had broken! I had been trying to look like a stud, peeling the sugarcane with my teeth, but ended up losing the bottom part of my front incisor!

She looked at me with those dark deep eyes and blushed. Her face betrayed two expressions — amusement at my chipped tooth and shyness. After a long pause, she flashed a million-dollar smile and said, 'I love you and want to be with you too!'

We have been married two years and still laugh every time we reminisce about my unusual proposal.

Abhay Chawla

Time Has Told

It was the 18th of May, 2009. No, it wasn't our wedding anniversary. However, my husband would be quick to respond, saying, 'It was the day I married you in my mind a year ago.'

Our third and decisive meeting in the arranged marriage process took place on 18th May, 2008. This was preceded by two consecutive meetings a month ago. I saw my husband for the first time when he came to my house as a marital prospect. I entered the guest lounge and there he was, sitting in the perfect straight-spine posture; giving me a warm, close-mouthed yet wide smile, the kind you wouldn't expect from a stranger. He was not a Brad Pitt lookalike and it was definitely not the cliché love-at-first-sight. When I asked him what is it that he was looking for in his would-be bride, he was clear about it. 'A good heart,' he said unlike my list of 2,918 characteristics required in my Prince Charming.

In the first two meetings, I subjected him to essay-type questions and he did justice to them by answering with vivid, thoughtful descriptions. On the contrary, I gave short and diplomatic answers to his questions, leaving them to his interpretation. This was not some evil strategy but my natural disposition towards inexpressiveness. At the end of two meetings, I was almost sure that he is a good human being and that with him, life would be an interesting and evolving journey. I was still a sweet, harmless mystery to him.

We met a month later for the third time. Yes, on the 18th of May, 2008. We had not communicated by any means during the period between the second and third 'date'. This gave both of us some time to retrospect — for him to do his consultant sort of research and analysis (he was a consultant with BCG) and for me to weigh costs against benefits (I had just completed my MBA, so I thought I might as well put theories into practice). All said and done, only a few issues needed to be clarified on both sides and if nothing went drastically wrong, it was probably going to be a yes-yes situation.

After half-an-hour of the 'question and answer session', there was silence. Impatient as I am about getting 'work' finished, I blurted out: 'I am okay, if you are okay.' Again there was silence, this time a more awkward one. He was looking at me in amazement, coupled with a grin. It was then that I realised I had actually proposed to him. He looked at his watch. It was 5:45 p.m. How rude, I thought to myself. Why on earth is he not saying anything? What is the grin about? Is he laughing at me? I was feeling stupid about my 'brave' act. After fifteen minutes, he said he was 'honoured'. Was it a euphemism for saying no, I wondered. As the clock struck 6:15 p.m., he took out a ring from his jacket, knelt down on his knees and slipped it onto my right hand finger (then, neither of us knew that the engagement ring is supposed to be worn on the left hand, a mistake corrected later). I was expecting a 'will you marry me?' on sight of the ring. But I realised I had already done the honours. He apologised for the wait and explained that his family believed in the *mahurat* which only started at 6:15 p.m.

Thus began our nine-month courtship. I was living in Ahmedabad and he was working in Mumbai. We were surviving on multiple phone conversations each day, in which I would do most of the talking, for a change. I think he had grasped by now that to get me talking, he would have to talk less and ask more questions. In the process of trying to fill the gap in communication, so as not to appear dumb, pun intended, I felt I was filling the void in my life by sharing it with someone. We would usually meet every other weekend. I would unfailingly drag him to watch Bollywood movies because I love them. He had always dressed in formals, but he started wearing jeans because I like casuals. We would go shopping, obviously because I love it. He would get me orchids and compose poems for me. He would ignore the newly sprouted zit on my face. He would tell me countless times that he loves me and the sceptic in me would romantically reply, 'Time will tell.'

I liked him in our courtship for the irritatingly righteous person that he is, but began to love him after we got married for selfish reasons. He takes care of little things to make sure I'm comfortable. He listens to the chaos of my emotions and dons the avatar of panacea. He brings clarity to my decisions and direction in life. He pushes me to grow as a person. And he surprises me just to see my eyes sparkle.

Three months after our 'official' wedding was our engagement anniversary. He had told me that he would have to go out of town for work. I was annoyed with him. But I knew something was amiss when our car did not turn towards the airport. After a couple of hours, we reached a palace hotel in Rajasthan. I was indulging in royalty, swimming in the pool attached to our room, being gifted with Swarovski earrings and being served a seven-course dinner. And then he wished me, 'Happy Anniversary, Darling.'

Smita Kothari

Will You Marry Me?

What Farid Khan thought...

She looked stunning. Everything about her was ethereal to me. I walked up to her, flashing my million dollar smile and gave her a bunch of roses. Escorting her to the table, I gallantly pulled out a chair for her. I tried to look cool but was far from it.

Maya and I had been together for a long time. We were made for each other. After three years of courtship, I finally decided to pop the question. But there was a problem. I wasn't sure if she wanted to marry me. I mean... I knew she liked me but what if she refused? I was a Pakistani Muslim and she was a Hindu. I knew this did not matter to her but... Did it? We had never really spoken about marriage. But I had to take this chance or I would never know.

I had prepared three ways of proposing to her and had rehearsed in front of the mirror a few hundred times. I would pick any one of the three, depending on her mood. My first idea was to get down on one knee, present the ring to her and ask, 'Will you marry me, Maya?' It would be a little dramatic, so I thought of another plan.

I would simply hold her hand and ask her, 'What do you think of becoming Mrs Maya Khan from Miss Maya Sharma?' But I didn't want to sound too confident. Something a little more light-hearted would work with Maya. So, as a third plan, I decided to pose a funny question like 'Can I be the grandfather to your grandchildren?' That was lame. Well, it had to be one of these. There was nothing else I could think of.

Maya was staring at me intently, sitting across the table. I could not judge her mood and was having a tough time deciding how to propose. She looked a little irritated and asked me, 'Is something wrong, Farid?'

'Nope, not at all... Why don't you order two chocolate milkshakes... And I will be back in a moment.' I got up and walked uneasily towards the restroom. Looking at the mirror, I cursed myself for acting like a fool. I splashed some water on my face and went back to the table. Maya looked peeved as I kept talking about the weather. She excused herself and went to the restroom and I was relieved to get a few moments to compose myself. The waiter arrived with the milkshakes. Without waiting for her to come back, I took a few sips to cool down. Just then, I had a remarkable idea.

What Maya Sharma thought...

I looked at Farid, wondering what in the world was wrong with him. He was definitely restless. He kept talking to himself and smiling as he walked to the restroom. But then, he had been acting a little strange lately. I went to the restroom to take a break from his odd behaviour. Something was weird but I went back to the table and decided to pretend like everything was alright.

The milkshake felt cool and refreshing after Farid's peculiarity. I had almost finished my drink when I spotted a glittering object at the bottom of the glass. I fished it out with a spoon. It was a ring! So, this was what the matter was! I stared at Farid who looked a little shaken up. His eyes spoke volumes as he kept quiet.

I cleaned the ring with the napkin and said, 'Farid Khan, why has it taken you three whole years to ask me this? Of course I will be your bride!'

What a silent spectator on a neighbouring table thought...

The young man suddenly looked relieved. It was almost as if he had regained his lost sanity. The young woman, who was calm and collected earlier, now blushed every time she eyed her beautiful ring. She batted her eyelids foolishly and slipped into a shy demeanour. Yes! It was definitely a proposal.

Meena N. Murugappan

3

IT'S JUST FOR YOU

Love does not consist of gazing at each other, but in looking together in the same direction.

–Antoine de Saint-Exupery

A Valentine's Job Offer Letter

My dear brand-new-husband,

I am pleased to inform you that I have decided to offer you the position of being my Valentine this year. My decision is based on your impressive performance in the past eight months.

Should you accept this offer, your salary will continue to be 730 square meals per year, payable in two daily instalments. Also included are perks like 365 plates of breakfast mixed with a generous scoop of affection and 745 cups of hot coffee. I shall continue to wash your soiled laundry and sew your shirt buttons. I trust that you will not refuse this generous offer.

You may be interested in knowing exactly why I arrived at this decision.

I remember the time when my Public Relations Officers (my parents) mentioned an advertisement under the matrimonial column. They sent an application to which you replied promptly, confirming that the position was still available. But before I could attend an interview to meet you, I got a job offer to work in the US. My father decided to bravely allow his daughter to go on this overseas mission. He assumed that with a visa in my hands, I would find plenty of other suitors. He then wrote to you.

Dear Mr S...,

We have decided to let our daughter follow her dreams and pursue a career abroad. We would not want to obstruct your own search for a suitable candidate. Please do not wait for us. Good bye and good luck!

Sincerely

Would've-been Father-in-law

In the meantime, you were approached by many worthy candidates. Luckily for me, you did not find any of them satisfactory. Do you remember that girl whose parents invited you over for an interview and kept feeding you with multiple plates of upma and jalebis? You were stuffed and you left in a huff as you did not want to marry into a family of gluttons.

Fortunately, I was not leaving India for the next two months. My mother rushed to your town to meet you and was delighted to find that you were still a confused, uh-um, confirmed bachelor. She returned home and filed this report:

'Six foot debonair gentleman; bespectacled; computer engineer; Bachelor's degree from *this* IIT; Master's degree from *that* IIT, returned to India after post-graduate fellowship in USA; owns his own computing firm; also owns a motorcycle!'

I fell in love instantly...with the motorcycle!

We then received your horoscope. Our constellations were a perfect match. I was now ready for a formal interview.

I was forced into wearing a pink Mysore silk saree with loads of jasmine flowers in my long braided hair. Professionally dressed to woo you, we marched into your apartment with confidence. There you were — shy, and very tall with thick glasses! We had barely exchanged a few words, but our silent dialogue was fruitful because we ended up getting married.

We fluttered around town as husband and wife on our 'scooter' (earlier misunderstood as a motorcycle). You drove me to Bombay Sweets for Dhokla and chutney and bought me fresh flowers every day.

The day came when I finally left for my job in the US with a heavy heart. We exchanged long-distance phone calls. Your letters were 'educational' with advanced chapters on planetary motion, written in your sweet attempts to instruct me on jet-lag, motion sickness and lack of sleep.

When overseas communication became tiresome, you decided to come to the US to your favourite student.

You were always very patient with me. You taught me driving with the help of that GPS system inside your head, and tolerated my cooking! You have always been a conservative listener, looking at me with blinking eyeballs, inquiring if I had actually said something. How sweet is that!

My Valentine Day's job offer is reserved exclusively for you. Your employment is effective immediately and will not be terminated at any time, or for any reason. Feel free to talk to me over dinner should you have any questions about our company.

P.S. Please don't forget to pick up some groceries for dinner this evening.

Here's the shopping list:

1. A gallon of non-fat milk. This is to keep you fit, my dear.
2. A bag of fresh green spinach. This is to keep you going, my dear.

3. A box of 'I-Can't-Believe-It's-Not-Butter'. This helps keep the diameter of a certain paunch under check.
4. A heart-shaped box of pastel pink candy along with a nice card addressed to your precious Valentine. Sky Blue won't work this time!

Sincerely Yours

The Loving Wife

P.S. This heartfelt assurance is your medical insurance!

Ranjini Sharma

An Addiction Called Love

Four years ago, on a muggy July evening, I got a call from my friend telling me, 'Book your tickets. Didi's marriage date is being fixed on Sept 1. Lots of work to be done.' It was news that made me instantly happy. Few weeks ago, Didi had come and stayed with me when she visited my city on an official tour. During her conversations with me, she used to check her mobile coyly to read SMSes. And in the mornings, she used to go to the balcony for taking a 'clear' call from abroad. Instincts told me that there's someone special in her life. But then I thought she herself should choose a moment to tell me.

She did that before going back to Delhi. She shared the story of how she came close to him and her excitement, joy and apprehension to start life in faraway Australia. But then love does strange things to one. It gives you wings to fly high and explore uncharted terrain. This is what happened to Didi. Before flying back to Delhi, she told me she would keep me posted on the developments. And she did keep her promise.

I arrived in Delhi just two days prior to the wedding. Didi's two independent and capable younger sisters were in full action, preparing for the wedding. No matter how much everybody teased them about their highly commendable 'jugaad' ability, they paid attention to every small detail. Not with a frown. But with lots of enthusiasm and happiness. All of us drove down together for a mehendi session and bangle shopping. The hard day came to a pleasant ending over a nice dinner at Sikkim House. And that was not the end of the story. In the middle of the night, my friend and I were driving around Delhi checking out hotel rooms and their tariffs so that Didi could spend her first night in *ishtyle*.

The wedding was arranged in a temple. So on the day of the wedding, we all chose our fine saris and salwar kameez to accompany the bride and the videshi bridegroom. Didi was looking resplendent in a traditional Manipuri dress. It was difficult to ignore that glow on her face. I chose to be with my friend on the long drive to the temple (we were lucky that day not to be caught in traffic jams). The temple was situated in a quiet place and the surroundings were beautiful. For us, it was a special moment as we were all in charge of the 'ceremony' management. And the 'core' group of women volunteers were all charged up. As the priest chanted the mantra, all of us showered flowers on the couple and wished for their happy married life. I promptly fished out my PAN card from my handbag as my identity proof for being a witness.

In the midst of all of us laughing and enjoying Didi's marriage, I could not help but notice one young couple getting married in the same premise, just a few steps away. The girl was dressed in a red synthetic salwar kameez and the boy was plainly dressed. There was no jewellery adorning the young girl. All that she was wearing was a dozen glass bangles. But she was looking very happy. Their only two witnesses (who were required to sign the papers) gave them company on one of the important days of their life. As I found out, they had eloped to get married, far from the prying eyes of their parents and relatives who were dead against the match. But they followed their heart.

In between running around to get photocopies of the PAN card and signing papers, I forgot about this young couple getting married. Then, as Didi's wedding ceremony got over, we all got into our cars to head to a restaurant in Connaught Place for a South Indian meal as the bridegroom loved southern delicacies.

With my friend behind the wheel, it's never a boring moment as she's an expert in passing scathing comments on everything and anything under the sun. As her car came to a halt, thanks to the red light, I just turned my face and saw the same young couple sitting in the auto with arms around each other. In that hired three-wheeler, their world looked so very complete and blissful. I just showed them the thumbs up sign and in return they gave me a warm smile and waved their hands. It was one of the briefest encounters of my life. Yet it warmed my heart. The red lights turned green and my friend's car zoomed past the auto. We left them behind, in their newly found heaven. And I realised that there's no greater leveller than love. There's no higher addiction than romance.

Deepika

Bride Forever

Girls like it, especially if they've never been married before — it's
the dress. Girls want a wedding, they don't want a marriage.
                                                    –Salman Rushdie

Marriage brings with it the thrill of shopping and I did mine
like a princess. The most important item on my list was my
bridal lehenga. After looking at almost a hundred, I selected
a beautifully embroidered bright red one. When I draped it
around myself, I experienced the immense joy of becoming a
bride. I wanted to look like the most gorgeous woman on the
planet that day.

Finally, the D-Day arrived. The wedding was taking place
in Gwalior, where my fiancé lived. My mother-in-law had
booked the best salon of the city for me.

Nothing can beat the pleasure of getting dressed as a bride
and along with my sister, I reached the salon dreamy-eyed.
To my shock, there were almost thirty brides sitting there! My
wedding date was supposed to be an auspicious one and it
seemed like all the spinsters of Gwalior were getting married
that same day! So here I was sitting amongst a horde of brides,

waiting for my turn to get dressed up. It felt like I was a part of a mass marriage ceremony!

As I sat and watched, I saw several girls getting transformed from ugly ducklings to beautiful swans. Suddenly, my sister got a call informing us that the baraat had arrived! And here I was, looking the ordinary girl next door.

My head started spinning and I yelled at the supervisor of the salon. She panicked and hastily started doing my make-up herself. I was too confused and nervous to even notice what she was doing. This was my biggest day and I was supposed to look like a million bucks! But it had all gone terribly wrong. The lady was finished with me in fifteen minutes and there was clearly nothing great about the way I looked. There was nothing I could do now.

As I walked towards the mandap, I felt all eyes were gaping at how commonplace I looked after keeping the groom and his family waiting for so long.

My heart was heavy but I forced a smile. The next moment I saw my groom walking towards me. He looked serious. 'Oh God! He is obviously as disappointed as I am,' I cringed.

As he came close to me, he swiftly bent forward and whispered in my ears, 'You're the best looking bride ever.'

I stared at him until my sister nudged me to look down. A smile spread on my face like a cool breeze and I forgot everything that had happened earlier in the day. That moment onwards, I felt like a superstar. Even my wedding pictures show how radiant I looked that day.

I may have been one of those thirty brides that day, but for my groom I was the only one! I was his bride forever!

So Mr Rushdie, what ultimately matters to a woman is to have a man who expresses his love for his woman with a smile on his lips and the truth in his eyes, all through life.

Roohi Bhatnagar

Celebrating A New-found
Home and Homeland!

Despite belonging to a community that doesn't celebrate Diwali with as much gusto as its own regional festivals, my Mumbai upbringing has ensured that I celebrate Diwali with great zeal and zest. Diwali to me not only meant a week-long vacation, but also everything that is typical of a Sooraj Barjatya or a Yashraj movie — loved ones and camaraderie amidst antakshari and dance, exchanging sweets and namkeens all decked up in bright clothes and jewellery, and traditional pujas and feasts in houses adorned with brightly lit diyas, lanterns and colourful rangolis.

Hence my excitement knew no bounds as Diwali was approaching and we were to fly from London, a city where I had moved to with my husband immediately after marriage, to join our friends and relatives back in India to celebrate my first Diwali as a newly-wed.

'Heartbroken' seemed to me like a mild word then, when my husband announced to me just a fortnight before we were to leave that we would not be in a position to visit India for

Diwali as some technical problem had come up in the project he headed, which needed him to be around. I was only half-hearing whatever he was saying as it was slowly dawning upon me that I was being asked to be away from a land where I had enjoyed twenty-six spirited Diwalis of my life... I was being asked to be away from everyone and everything that my mind associated with the word 'celebration'.

As the days passed by, dejection slowly assumed the form of guilt and then gradually envy as Diwali frenzy forcefully threw itself on me every time I switched on any of the Indian television channels. I sunk deeper into depression. After brooding and sulking endlessly, I gave up. I could take it no longer. I did not want to let the festivity pass without having my share of fun.

'So what if I can't be home,' I started thinking. 'The festival has earned a global appeal,' I consoled myself, somehow strangely. 'If the House of Commons in London can resemble India through their official celebrations on Diwali, if there can be a carnival at the Trafalgar Square on the occasion of Diwali, if Diwali can be the biggest festival outside India in Leicester with a main street which gets lit with hundreds and thousands of lights, why then can't I celebrate it at a home away from home,' I convinced myself.

A home away from home! With that very thought, an alien country and a house in a foreign land suddenly transformed into 'my very own abode'. I realised that even though this was not my mother's house or my mother-in law's, where a new bride would be pampered and spoilt on her first Diwali, I still had reasons to be happy, for this was a home that welcomed me, a nervous new bride into its comfort and which therefore rightly deserved the joy of my first celebration. I knew that this was certainly not the place that held my memories, but also came to accept that this could very well be the place where I could create new ones.

I fondly recalled that this was the very home where I had set foot after marriage, my eyes welling with love as my husband welcomed me with a traditional lamp in his hand. It had moved me deeply then to see that he had daintily arranged a silver plate on the doorstep that held wet vermillion which smeared my feet with its deep red to leave footprints as I walked into the house even as he showered grains of basmati rice on me, happy in the ignorance that they were the finest and the costliest variety of grains.

I looked around and realised that this was the very home within the walls of which I saw my marriage blossoming amidst coffee and candid conversations; a home where every piece of furniture unravelled a story of the bitter-sweet arguments between my husband and I over the pounds to be shelled out before we would bring a piece home; a home where every utensil clinked with the nostalgia of my careful scrutiny as I chose it to be a part of my sacred space; a home which although was a part of a land that was alien to us, but which still held close to its heart the memories of our togetherness.

As I recalled those beautiful moments, I felt everything around me brightening up. I went around the city with full gusto, crazily shopping and picking whatever goodies I could in a land that I now accepted to be my very own.

I made some quick calls and there we were, nine Indian couples gathered together to share recipes and churn out delicacies amidst gossip and friendly banter. In fact, it still gives me goose bumps to recall that together with my bunch of 'crazy new-found relatives with like minds', we went on to organise a community gathering and a mass Lakshmi Puja, to recreate in my own lawn the atmosphere of my homeland.

My first Diwali after marriage will always be special... Not only because I celebrated it with much verve than ever before... But because it matured me to a new realisation, that celebration never comes looking for an address.

Divya R.K.N. Nair

Flowers

Flowers are an essential part of every wedding, but in my marriage ceremony, they were almost like a living entity.

My bridegroom was allergic to the fragrance of flowers which is why we had to reluctantly settle for minimal fresh flowers for decorating my marriage hall. But on the wedding day, he succumbed to his mother's insistence on wearing a long façade of flower strings, as the sehra that would be tied to his forehead. I was ornamented with jasmine buds in my hair and wrists which was disappointing as they messed up my gorgeous hairstyle. I had a sehra too, that veiled my face, making all that effort on make-up futile. Yusuf was troubled by the countless flower strings dangling on his face. His head ached and eyes reddened with pain but he continued to smile, and greeted the guests for five agonising hours.

The ceremony was an ordeal and I could hardly wait for my bridegroom to take me home in a car beautifully adorned with flowers, in keeping with the tradition. We approached the moment of bidai, when the bride finally says goodbye to her parents, and the car that Yusuf had brought pulled up into the driveway. To my disbelief, the car was bare. For an instant I wanted to scream. I was terribly upset especially because Yusuf was aware of my fascination for this particular custom. I stifled my complaint even though my wedding day had been far from the divine experience I had imagined it to be.

The next day we left for our honeymoon to Thailand. As soon as we got a cosy Saomi Beach to relax, I spilled out my suppressed emotions and to my surprise, started crying. Yusuf was shocked to see my tears. He had obviously expected me to be considerate about his aversion.

'You wore flowers all through the wedding and were surrounded by them. Then how would flowers on a car bother you?' I sobbed uncontrollably before drifting off to sleep. I had been deprived of a privilege at the most precious moment of my life.

We had a wonderful trip although I missed my parents and lamented occasionally about my deprivation. The holiday was over in no time and we arrived at Indira Gandhi International Airport. The wait for the luggage was endless and Yusuf looked restless by the time it came. He rushed out to hail a taxi while I waited inside impatiently. Within a few minutes, he was back and at long last we were ready to leave.

'Let's go to our own home as husband and wife,' he held my hand lovingly and flashed a charming smile. I forgot all my woes.

He pulled me gently towards the exit and there it was! I held my breath to see a long swanky car decked with blooms of all varieties and colours. The flowers smiled from the roof and peeped mischievously through the windows, and a message read 'Just Married' on a heart-shaped bed of fresh, red roses! I had to pinch myself because I thought I could hear strains of my favourite song *Baharon phool barsao, mera mehboob aaya hai.* It was not a dream as I looked around to find three musicians standing in a corner and playing the song melodiously.

Yusuf took me by my hand into that beautifully decorated, chauffeur-driven car. I was overwhelmed and speechless as tears kept rolling down my cheeks.

Rana Siddiqui Zaman

Proving Dadi Right

'Mark my words, I will be his bride someday,' she always said it with such confidence. I was one of the few die hard romantics who believed her! I knew my friend Sonam and also knew how she always got what she wanted. Post college, we barely kept in touch and forgot all about Jaideep, the handsome young Turk, who lived in the mansion across the road from college.

Eight years later, I was having dinner with Sonam and it was like we were back in college. That's what is wonderful about old friends, you can pick up the threads like the years in between didn't happen. I told her all about my life in Mumbai and how exciting my career was. She, of course, didn't need to fill me in on details as far as her work went as she was a successful model and had clearly done better than most of us. What was lovely was that she had developed no airs or fake accents. She was also as hyper and as much of a perfectionist as she had been in college. She asked all about my husband and our life together. She was genuinely interested in what I was saying and I could tell that she was happy for me. By the time we were half way through the second wine bottle, she suddenly said she had something to tell me. She was keeping her word and marrying Jaideep. The money bags Jaideep, who was on the cover of the latest issue of *Business Today*. The guy she had a crush on ever since she was eighteen.

Maybe it was the wine that made me candid, but I had to know all the juicy details. They had met a year ago at a yoga class and the chemistry was instant. She didn't want a casual fling and that was what he had in mind. He couldn't possibly marry a model. She fought back tears as she told me how hard it was to stay away but she wasn't willing to settle for just an affair. The small town girl came to the fore...

He also realised that she wasn't the dumb bimbette he had thought she was. She also wasn't a gold digger like he feared. Yet they both knew how tough things were. She was just a girl wanting to be with the man she loved. Thankfully, he understood that and after much deliberation, popped the question. Of course, his family was horrified.

A month later, I got a call from Sonam. The wedding was in a week. His family had agreed and she was on tenterhooks. She needed me in Delhi.

Once I reached, I realised how stressed she was. Everything had to be perfect and the in-laws had to see that their son wasn't making a mistake. The project had to work. Everything was on a war footing and she was calling the shots. Each of us was assigned duties and we had meetings morning and evening to mark the progress. She was like a woman possessed and her focus was amazing. If she could, she would have ordered the weather for the day as well!

Her mother was upset at how this girl was driving around town all day and wouldn't do anything that brides-to-be did. Yet, we got it, as her friends. She told Jaideep that she would only see him at the wedding. From the venue, to the menu, to the flowers, to the music, Sonam was overseeing every detail. Her friends were wonderful. Designers, hoteliers, make-up experts. Everyone knew and loved her. All of us wanted her dream to be just right.

She was physically tired and taking this project too seriously. Never had any bride scrutinised mehendi designs with such clinical precision. Finally, two days before the wedding, as she was yelling at her designer pal, he gave it off to her. Amidst tears and hugs, we all yelled at her and asked her to calm down and enjoy her wedding. Nothing would go wrong. She looked baffled and stopped in her tracks. She was marrying a man who loved her — not going for the Miss Universe pageant. Someone had to say it and I did. She looked lost and vulnerable.

She looked radiant on the morning of her wedding. Jaideep sent her orchids and her favourite brownies. Yet, we could sense how tense she still was. While the ceremonies were on, she was making sure we updated her on her blackberry. She would nod or smile to acknowledge each message. We joked about how she would make the perfect CEO for one of Jaideep's companies.

While her make-up was being touched up and jewellery worn, we were all reporting in on the progress at every front. She finally said a silent prayer and left for the venue.

They made a lovely couple and he was clearly crazy about her. She was accepting the compliments graciously, yet her mind was racing at thousand thoughts a minute. She was anything but coy and finally I had to whisper in her ear that deep breathing is what was needed. The guests couldn't stop praising the arrangements and the food.

Her in-laws were suitably impressed. His grandmother blessed them saying she was the best bride her grandson could ever have got. Sonam's eyes moistened on hearing that. She's been proving Dadi right for the last five years...

Shifa Maitra

Waiting

Varsha glanced through her emails disinterestedly. Her inbox never had anything exciting in it. However, a mail from a stranger by the name of snobby_robby@yahoo.co.in caught her eye. As she clicked it open, it read…

'When a boy wants to see you everyday... he wants to be yours 4eva.

When a boy says 'I love you' ... he means it.

When a boy says 'I miss you' ... no one in this world can miss you more.

Make sure you spend your life with the right person...

Find a guy who will stay awake just to watch you sleep...

Send this to fifteen people to find your true love really soon!'

Varsha was clueless about who snobby_robby was, but found herself foolishly believing in his words. In no time, she had forwarded the message to fifteen friends. If it really works, the boy who would stay awake just to watch her sleep would soon breeze into her life.

She stepped out of her room and pinched herself. There was an attractive young boy standing in her balcony. This was really prompt!

'Varsha, this is Singhania Uncle. He has come back to India after ten years.' She was taken by surprise as her mother introduced her to an elderly gentleman sitting in their living room. She greeted him halfheartedly as it was the boy in the balcony who had her attention.

'That is my son, Mayank,' said Singhania Uncle to a visibly embarrassed Varsha, who smiled sheepishly and hurried into her room.

She was trying to concentrate on her homework, when there was a knock on her door.

'May I come in?' It was Mayank. He looked clearly bored and Varsha felt guilty about leaving him in the company of the elders.

'Sure. I was just struggling with trigonometry,' she replied, trying her best to sound indifferent.

'Allow me,' said Mayank, pulling the notebook towards him. Within seconds, he had cracked the sum as Varsha looked at him in awe. 'It is really simple,' he explained trigonometry to her the way Tripathy Sir never could. Math had never been so uncomplicated before. Varsha was almost convinced that sobby_robby was a genius!

Varsha and Mayank were soon spending most of their time together. It was almost like a wonderful dream. But her reverie was interrupted when her mother announced that Saxena Aunty and her nephew would be coming to see her this Sunday. The last couple of years of her life had revolved around Mayank. She never cared if there were other boys on earth and never even realised that she had turned into a beautiful woman. Varsha panicked and rushed to Mayank's office.

'Wow! This is great news! You are really going to get married?' Mayank reacted joyfully. He was obviously joking. 'Varsha, you are my dearest friend and I am truly happy for you.'

'Friend'! The word hit her like lightning as it snapped her out of her delusion. She realised that they had spent time together but Mayank had never told her that he loved her. He bought her friendship bands, but had never said that some day he would buy her a diamond ring too. He had spent nights talking to her, but had never promised that he would spend his entire life with her. Varsha had been living a fairy tale that she had spun for herself. With a broken heart, she dragged herself back home.

Within a week, her house came alive with her wedding preparations and soon, it was the big day. Varsha was totally unaware how gorgeous she looked in her bridal finery. She did not seem to care.

'You look really tired,' said Aditya on the wedding night, trying to break the ice. Varsha was quiet. 'Tomorrow we have a puja and you will have to get up at 5 a.m. It is past midnight, I guess you should go off to sleep now,' said the new groom to his beautiful bride. Varsha silently heaved a sigh of relief. Aditya seemed like a pleasant guy but was he anything like the boy in the email? She drifted off to sleep with several apprehensions in her heart.

When Varsha woke up the next morning, she was surprised to see that Aditya was not there in the room. She noticed a pink paper on the coffee table. Her eyes brimmed with tears as she read the note: 'I am going to the temple. You can come later with mom. And just wanted to let you know... You look beautiful while asleep. I couldn't stop myself from staring at you the entire night, and I can do this all my life. I know you may take time to be comfortable with me. It's okay. I can wait.'

'But I can't,' thought Varsha.

She had waited for a very long time. After all, this was the man she had awaited for eight golden years of her life.

Avantika Debnath

Wisdom of the Decision

Our teacher, Mrs Vaidehi Dutt, was born and brought up in a rich but orthodox family. Though there was a little relaxation in family restrictions as far as her education was concerned, she was sent to a girls' school, a girls' college and unfortunately at the university, she only had girls in her class. Being a good student, she was allowed the privilege of studying thus far. Soon after her post-graduation, her parents decided to marry her off. As part of the family custom, her parents chose a match for her. Though she got an opportunity to meet her would-be in-laws, she was not allowed to meet the bridegroom.

At last the wedding day arrived. Vaidehi was initially very depressed about the fact that she was not given the freedom to choose her own life partner. The idea of an arranged marriage seemed to contradict the romantic fantasies she had about her soulmate. She envied her friends who had the liberty of choosing their own boyfriends who could later on become their husbands.

Vaidehi was decked up in jewellery that was inherited by the family and was worn as a symbol of the rich tradition they had. She was a good-looking young woman with a glimmer of soft emotion and innocence in her beautiful brown eyes, and the gold ornaments added to her elegant and glamorous look.

All the while Vaidehi thought of revolting against the practice that was imposed by her family members. She felt as if she would be drowned in the eternal gloom of dissatisfaction that was below her level of consciousness. On second thoughts, she realised that her rebellion would lead to unnecessary sorrow and pain for her near and dear ones. She decided to accept their wish as her fate. Gradually, her feeling of unconscious retaliation was overwhelmed by her curiosity to meet her husband. She wondered what he would look like and, importantly, what kind of person he would be. She hoped that her family had considered all these things before judging a person to be an ideal life partner for her. As far as she knew her parents, they never paid attention to such details. Perhaps the only thing that they were interested in was a conservative and aristocratic family like theirs.

Finally the moment arrived when the bride and the bridegroom would see each other for the first time at an auspicious moment (known as Shubho Drishti in Bengali custom) that would be followed by the wedding ceremony. Vaidehi covered her face with a betel leaf as per the custom. At last, she was asked to remove it and see her husband. She could hardly believe that the time had arrived when all her speculations would come to an end and she would actually come face to face with her husband. She could hear her heart beat fast in anticipation of something that may or may not seem to be strange. Her eyes and his met as they looked at each other. He seemed to be a handsome man and had a mischievous twinkle in his eyes. His porcelain skin glowed as he smiled, and his black hair was neatly combed. She found a great deal of warmth and affection radiating from his sparkling black eyes, which made her feel comfortable and secure.

'I feel as if I know him since ages. How's it possible? This is the first time that I am seeing him,' Vaidehi told her aunty who was standing next to her.

'It is possible. There is a saying that husband and wife meet each other consecutively for seven births,' her aunty explained.

'So you mean to say that this is my fifth or sixth birth with him? Perhaps this is the reason I feel that he is a known face,' Vaidehi said thoughtfully.

Soon the wedding ceremony started. Vaidehi felt as if her feeling of discontent was whipped off by her husband's winsome smile, but her mind was still occupied by the thought of the recently evolved question relating his identity.

'Did you recognise me?' Vaidehi's husband whispered into her ears all of a sudden in the midst of the ceremony.

She was extremely puzzled and wondered why he had asked such a question when they had never met before. She seldom had the opportunity to meet any man privately in her life as she was always escorted by her family members whenever she would attend any function or a ceremony, and it was next to impossible to meet a boy in a girls' school, college or university. She would often compare herself with the heroine Miranda of Shakespere's famous play *The Tempest*. Her life was similar to that of Miranda, without an opportunity to meet a man and perhaps this was the reason she was fascinated by the hero

Ferdinand on their very first encounter on the lonely island on which she and her father were stranded for twelve years. Similarly, Vaidehi thought that she had fallen in love with her husband at first sight.

Vaidehi could not fathom the reason her husband mentioned the word 'recognise' when she had not seen him earlier. She tried hard to jog her memory but all her efforts were in vain. She tried to think of other places where she might have come across him. She remembered that when she was a teenager, her father used to take her along to their sweet shop at Park Street. She used to spend hours together watching her father monitor the work of their employees. At times she did get to see customers who were full of praise for the quality of sweets that was sold out and occasionally they would come up to her father to thank him in person. Suddenly she remembered a teenage boy who would accompany his grandfather to their shop. They generally purchased around ten kilos of sweets whenever they visited them. The teenage boy seemed to be very charming. She wished in her heart that she would have a boyfriend like him. She envied her friends who would often proudly mention their boyfriends, who were in comparison nowhere near to this adorable boy. Though the boy never spoke to her, he would always smile at her, which she felt (at that point of time) was a sense of gratitude for the high quality products that they delivered. It seemed as if this boy resembled her husband in some way. He was indeed the same person who had grown up into a handsome man! Her spirit exulted as she finally got an answer to the question that occupied her mind for so long. Her happiness knew no bounds and her respect for her parents increased with the realisation that they were undeniably her true well wishers.

The wedding ceremony ended after some time. They were led to another room where the custom of meeting family members started.

At an opportune moment, she whispered into her husband's ears, 'I have recognised you.'

'Really! Then tell me who am I,' he asked.

'You are my soulmate,' Vaidehi smiled at him.

Sreelekha Chatterjee

4

THE PERFECT DRESS

After all there is something about a wedding-gown prettier than in any other gown in the world.
—Douglas William Jerrold

Dressing Up the Bride

We had a court marriage in the morning. I went to the beauty parlour to get ready for our reception in the evening. Despite my anxiety, I kept a broad smile on my face.

I had never ever really dressed up. I was not vain about my good looks or even good looking enough to be vain, but just happy to be myself, without any outside help. My husband had declared that he liked me the way I was. But my parents insisted and I had to admit that I had never attended a wedding where the bride was not dressed for the occasion.

As soon as I sat down, the ladies started fussing over me. I wasn't used to this, but decided to allow myself to be pampered the way a bride is supposed to be. Hours passed by as layers of make-up were applied to my face. My nails were painted and my hair was pulled around, sprayed and twisted into a strange looking coil. It was a harrowing experience and I found it increasingly difficult to recognise myself in the mirror. After the job was done, the team stepped back and looked at me like I was an expensive work of art.

I rushed home. It was late and soon my husband would be there to pick me up for our reception.

'How do I look, Ma?' I asked mom as soon as I entered the house.

'Like a bride,' she replied proudly.

At last, I was beginning to feel good about myself. Just then my dapper husband stepped in. Even while I was admiring how handsome he looked in a suit, I noticed how his jaw dropped as he looked at me. Soon enough he found his voice.

'What have you done to yourself?'

'I…er…you don't like it?' I asked hesitantly.

'I can't even recognise you. You look so much better without this stuff,' he remarked with a horrified look on his face.

The next sequence of events happened really fast as I pushed everyone out of the room, removed my saree and locked myself in the bathroom. I showered and scrubbed my face, neck and shoulders. I shampooed away all the sticky stuff in my hair. In a record time of ten minutes, I came out with a towel wrapped around my head, totally cleansed. Draping the saree, I put on some jewellery and a red bindi. I towel-dried my hair, combed it and stepped out nervously.

My husband looked at me and holding my hand guided me to the car. Somewhere along the way, he whispered that I was looking unbelievably beautiful.

I blushed happily, glowing and feeling more beautiful and special than I ever had in my life. My husband did like me the way I was!

Irene Dhar Malik

My Shaadi ka Lehenga

My lehenga was carefully unwrapped from the mul cloth I keep it wrapped in, with the cloves to keep silverfish at bay, and the faint musty smell of something precious and stored. Yup, after I'd fallen to the ground and had old shoes brought to revive me when I caught a glimpse of the choli which I must have definitely stitched in infant size as there was no way even half of me was hoping to fit self into the entire whole of it, I realised it had been a while since I'd actually taken it out to look at. Could it be possible that once upon a time I actually had arms that were matchsticks? You know. I could have been a stick insect and I never appreciated it. Arms that could be left bare in sleeveless tees and trusted not to jiggle themselves into the shimmy shake if all one attempted was an innocent bye-bye gesture. Well. All that really means is that yours truly is never ever going to be able to do the red carpet walk and wave, but then, who really wants to. After all, yours truly is never going to be invited on said red carpet anyway, except perhaps to lay it out. The red carpet that is. What did you think?

Speaking of red, the lehenga is red. Brilliant red. In true blue

North India style. With embroidery so heavy I almost had to be propped up at my reception with cousins and quick swigs of alcohol. Of course I'm kidding. I didn't need the cousins to prop me up, I didn't have any who would have taken on the task of propping me up, given that no one was willing to risk life and limb to be splatted under falling bride. Seriously though, given the size of them arms, I must have been chicken proportions when I wore said lehenga. It was a wonder I didn't fall in a crumpled heap to the floor. Would have been nice though, bride-like swoon, considering one made a most unseemly bride with not the remotest smidgeon of any trace of tears during the bidai. I am reminded of, by the spouse, of my unseemly glee in hurrying to the honeymoon suite booked at close by hotel, though I insist it was an urgency to use the facilities which one was unable to with gazillion swarming guests oohing and aahing over one. Brides are not supposed to pee. Right. They have to smile and look radiant, and not need to clean their teeth post dinner with toothpicks.

The lehenga is gorgeous. It has huge paiseleys in gold gota. Sequins splashed liberally all over, and buckram lining the hem of the skirt to keep the flare out. It is no designer label, just a regular model picked up from Mumbai's Gandhi market. There we were, me tripping over the massive floor sweeping length of the lehenga, wincing at the shoe bites from the new pair of shoes bought especially for the function, at the five star hotel where we had a room booked for us by a kind aunt for our suhaag raat. Of course, we couldn't afford five star hotel rooms, we earned pittances. You noticed me wincing with the unspeakable pain being inflicted on me by shoe bites and slowed down your pace to mine. I had, of course, yet to experience childbirth. I had a zero pain threshold back then. And when we entered the room, you did the metaphoric un-Indian ritual of carrying me over the threshold. If you threw your back out with the effort, you didn't complain. And then, wedding lehengas are not the easiest garments to divest oneself of, especially when one is half asleep on one's feet. And one realises that the hair is now a mass of solidified concrete, with hairspray made of something so lethal one would have to take a pickaxe to get all the hair pins out of the backcombed beehive. You sat down, patiently, with the handshower, and got me to put my head in the basin while you washed out the concrete-hold hair spray and made me feel human again. You helped me out of the lehenga, the infinite bangles I was wearing, the jewellery I was loaded with, and tucked me into bed. I was exhausted and dozed off in a second. That's been a pattern, hasn't it, a pattern set from day one of our wedding. I hyperventilate, you calmly resolve the issue. You may never say 'I love you', or do the flowers and hearts routine, but your actions reassure me more than words ever could.

Airing the lehenga out brought back memories of standing next to the newly acquired spouse, accepting gifts and envelopes and wondering what they contained, and not knowing one would get around two dozen steel utensils and three lemonade sets, and the gift opening ceremony would be something that you would have happily traded for the pleasure of watching paint dry given the wow quotient of gifts that emerged from those wrappings. That of the fluttering in the stomach as I wondered what turn my life would now take. The lehenga, to me, is a symbol of the day my life changed completely the first time round.

I aired out said lehenga, noticed the fading and blackened gota work with a wry smile. It has been thirteen years in the keeping, save for occasional airings and oohing and aahing with no practical use for it. Folded it, stuffed in cloves and wrapped it back in mul again. By next year, I think the waist too will seem impossible to get into. I will keep it as an heirloom for the grandchildren to play 'dress up' with. Now, why does that thought make me happy?

Kiran Manral

My Wedding Dress

It was at the impressionable age of nineteen that I got engaged to be married. I was shocked at myself and so were my friends in college. But I was floored by Ravi as soon we met, and to my parents' delight, agreed to marry him.

I was as juvenile as one could be at that age and took a foolish vow to get married in my favourite pair of Wrangler jeans. My mom obviously refused to hear anything about this. My dad would indulge me and then throw his hands up in the air and declare that he could do nothing about it. That made me more defiant. The fun was in breaking the rules and going against tradition. I had made tall claims to my friends about it and that is the way it would be! Ravi humoured me by saying that he would marry me irrespective of what I wore.

During one shopping excursion, I fell in love with a beautiful crystal studded bridal lehenga. My mom ignored my frail resistance and promptly bought it. The commitment to my jeans was weakening and my reputation was at stake. Determination turned into dilemma. My brother was excited and even placed bets with my cousins, and they all eagerly awaited the drama.

The big day finally arrived and I developed cold feet. My parents knew it all the while as I willingly dressed up in my wedding attire. But the jeans lying on the bed beckoned me. It was time to make my grand appearance.

I stepped out in my bridal finery. All my cousins rejoiced while my little brother looked betrayed. I glanced at him and winked and lifted my lehenga, just enough to give him a glimpse of the jeans I was wearing under it. He beamed with joy. I was happy that it made my naughty brother a little rich, I was happier that I could save face in front of my friends!

Even today, more than twenty years later, we break into side-splitting laughter every time we talk about it! And if you are wondering, yes, I still have that pair of jeans in my almirah.

Rajika Malhotra

Perfect

Perfect. Just like every other bride, that is how I wanted my wedding day to be.

My wedding trousseau was in place. The lady who would apply mehendi for me and the beauticians who would make me look like a million bucks were the best in the business, and I had booked their dates two months in advance. Everything was perfectly planned.

It was just two more days to the wedding and my house shimmered with colourful blinking lights and sun-kissed marigolds hanging from the balcony. I hummed melodious romantic songs and opened the new Echolac suitcase to pack my trousseau. Just then the phone rang. It was Miss Meena from the mehendi parlour.

'I am really sorry, but there has been a death in my family. I will not be able to come for the ceremony. But don't worry, I will send my sister-in-law, Devaki. She is as good as I am,' said an apologetic Miss Meena. I hung up unhappily and hoped that Devaki would be at least half as good as Miss Meena.

She turned out to be far from half as good and I cried

bitterly after seeing the mess that my mehendi was. As I stared outside the window of my room, occasionally glancing at my disastrous mehendi, I felt a hand on my shoulder. It was Mother. She hugged me and I could feel her touch telling me that everything would be fine.

The next morning was officially my last day at my parents' house... At my house I scanned the walls, the furniture, the wall hangings and the photographs. Everything seemed to talk to me. I felt a tug in my chest and choked. I never realised how much these meant to me. The phone kept ringing all morning with relatives calling to offer their help with everything that should not have mattered to them. All of a sudden, my younger sister barged in and informed me that Rita had got the measles. Rita was the lady who was to make me look like a million bucks!

I ran to Mother and stared at her with my teary eyes. She looked calm. I wondered how she handled all the pressure.

'Don't worry sweetheart, your eyes will become puffy with so much crying. I have already arranged for a replacement. Sheila aunty will come to dress you up. She is very good.'

Of course! If she was anything like Miss Meena's sister-in-law, my wedding day would be perfect... A perfect disaster! Tears continued to stream down my cheeks. 'Things could have been worse, honey. Come and let us all have some breakfast, please,' Mother consoled me. It was the last breakfast with my family before I was married.

'What did you feel when you were getting married? You were just twenty!' I asked Mother.

'Well, that my father's house was only a hop, skip and jump away from my husband's house and I could visit my parents

whenever I felt like!' replied Mother, as she smiled with
dimples denting her cheeks on both sides. We all had a good
laugh, making light of the moment. But then there was silence
as Mother spoke again.

'But that is not all that I felt. Marriage is much more than just
ceremonies. It is pious. Marriage is about love, about raising
a family and supporting it through good and bad times. Your
mehendi, make-up and trousseau will be forgotten soon. It is
how you conduct yourself in your new life that will matter.
And I am sure you will do us proud!' The Parle G that I dipped
in my hot coffee broke away. I felt frivolous and juvenile. What
was I thinking, howling over make-up and the works? That
night I did not sleep. I did not want to leave my parents, my
sisters and my house. Marriage was not only about the tinkle
in the bangles, the mystic red of my wedding sari, or the glitter
in my diamond jewellery. I knew it was more. I had been on
cloud nine ever since I fell in love with my best friend and we
had vowed to spend the rest of our lives together. But the pain
of separating from my roots and Mother's summation of my
life that was about to begin in the next few hours made me see
things differently. I felt foolish and cried myself to sleep.

It was D-day. We reached the wedding venue early for some
rituals before the actual ceremony. Soon after the puja, Sheila
aunty and her assistant started working on me like craftsmen.
Not wanting to look at the mirror, I closed my eyes and thought
of Mother, Dad and my little sisters. I was going to miss them.

'I am done,' announced Sheila aunty as she pinned the veil
delicately over my forehead and added finishing touches to
my red bindi and lipstick. She asked me to stand and turn
towards the mirror.

As I opened my eyes, I saw Mother standing right behind me, like always. But this time, she was crying. She held my hand and whispered in my ears: 'You look perfect today, just as I had always imagined. Perfect!'

Vaishali Shroff

The Perfect Dress

I was a very happy bride. All brides are happy... Well, usually, but I was an exception to the extent that all I had cared about in the months preceding my wedding was that I was going to spend the rest of my life with this wonderful person I'd met and fallen for in an instant.

What I need to explain here is that this marriage was what is termed 'love marriage' in our country — a union of two distinctly and culturally opposite poles — a Marwari (me!) and a Tam-Bram (Tamilian Brahmin, my husband!).

Under Marwari traditions, not only was I supposed to be given a sizeable dowry (how I cringe at that word!), but my cartload of relatives were also to be given gifts — in cash or kind.

I was twenty-one, madly in love and totally oblivious to the shopping sprees and hectic activity that surrounded the wedding. I had no clue what I was going to wear, what my parents were buying as gifts (for me as well as others) and what would happen on that day.

I spent all the time I had dreaming about being with this man... The nitty gritties of the wedding were just nitty gritties to me, left to the others to handle. All I did was concentrate on eating papaya to get an 'internal' glow on my skin and try to lose some weight before D-Day.

My aunts and mom (in that order) plotted, planned and executed the shopping — my clothes, jewellery and even purses! In fact, as soon as I moved into my home with my husband as a newly-wed, the first thing I did was throw away the atrocious golden, bronze and silver coloured purses!

While I lived in a dream-like state of moony nirvana, things were being finalised around me.

To our utter surprise, the groom and his parents converged at our home (the designated venue for the traditional wedding rituals) at 5.30 a.m. or so to begin the ceremonies. I was rudely woken up and was requested to desist from stepping out of my room as the ceremony had begun in our living room!

Now remember this was a time when mobile phones did not exist. As my home filled up with relatives before the wedding, it became impossible for the to-be husband and I to catch up on the landline. Strangely, he was as inattentive to the ceremonial calendar as I was and we never discussed the finer details of the wedding — ever!

All we knew (the bride's side i.e.) was that the actual ceremony would begin at 8.30 a.m. The 5.30 a.m. sudden thronging of the groom's family was a shock to all of us! But my parents did the best they could — took quick showers and organised tea, coffee, breakfast as the groom's family sat around a pyre that brought tears to every eye in the household.

After the brahmanical pre-wedding rites, it was time for me to join the coterie 'dressed up' in a nine-yard saree.

As per Tam-Bram customs, this was compulsory and although I didn't know when my mother had managed to get me one, I knew from the start that this was going to be one mean ride!

It was at the nth hour (a few minutes before I was to be seated at the 'mandapam') that we realised that I had not stocked up on the customary head jewellery (another MUST in the Tam-Bram system), hairpins to hold my step-cut hair in place (which had to be bedecked in flowers) and even enough safety pins!

My brothers ran helter-skelter to buy these things — safety pins, hairpins, jewelled head gear and flowers (driving to the nearby market and hoping as hell that one of the knick knack stores would be open at 8 a.m.) and chaos reigned as aunts and cousins laboured over the bride, trying to dress her up!

Some of my close friends who had come for the wedding had to part with their pins (safety and hair) for the bride.

To the dismay of the 'dressing up group', they also discovered that ignorant of the fact that nine-yard sarees don't have falls, my mother had a fall, not stitched, but peekoed on!

Some of my cousins were aghast that I had chosen not to get dressed or made up by a professional on the most important day of my life... And furthermore, I hadn't even had a dress or make-up rehearsal before the auspicious day!

The flurry of activity did hassle me out a bit, but not as much as the 'dressing up group' who tried so hard to make me look like a bride and not a dancer after a long show with messed up, unkempt hair and what not!

All this happened even as the elders of the family insisted that we were running out of the 'mahurat' time and the groom sat outside anxiously waiting for his bride.

When I walked out, the nine-yard saree draped on me with the 'fall' visible on the outer layer, I don't know what went on in other minds, but I was back in the state of nirvanic bliss... Glad that we would finally be able to get on with the ceremony which would unite us in bonds of matrimony forever!

I have several pictures of my 'fiasco' wedding in terms of dressing (and the 'fall' is noticeable in each of them) but given a chance, I know I would do it very much the same way again.

Ritu Goyal Harish

5

THE BIG DAY

I dreamed of a wedding of elaborate elegance,
A church filled with family and friends.
I asked him what kind of a wedding he wished for,
He said one that would make me his wife.

–Unknown

A Bridal Chamber

'Daddy, this is between you and me, please.'

Dad was so anxious I might vanish without a trace that I had to let him know where my husband Joe and I planned to spend our wedding night.

After scouting around for a romantic spot, I booked a room in a shiny new hotel overlooking the River Mandovi, upstream from Goa's capital city, Panjim. The hotel was the latest venture of Dad's dear friend, Vishnubhai, and I was glad to secretly contribute to his profits.

Secrecy was the operative word. This was one piece of information the clan could do without. An affectionate horde of friends and relations would turn up in Goa around the wedding date. My teenaged kin were the sort who could charm the hotel staff and gain entry to the bridal chamber before we did. An unlucky cousin and his bride had been subjected to an off-key midnight rendition of *Obladi! Oblada*!

After the ceremony, my relatives did what they could to make Joe feel welcome. An aunt informed him that he was now married to the family. While other guests showered flower petals on the newly-weds, the cousins flung fistfuls of petals as missiles. I had to shield my face with the bridal bouquet.

'Tell us where you are going,' said one of them. 'We've chartered a bus and have to give the driver directions.'

Joe, a fighter pilot, seemed unfazed at the prospect of much ragging. The Air Force had accustomed him to strange nuptial customs, from cornflakes under the mattress to full-blown kidnappings.

We seemed to have escaped detection as we drove away. But doubts arose when we arrived at the hotel and were led, not to the room I had booked, but to the honeymoon suite. There were vases of fresh flowers everywhere. It was a corner suite. Wide picture windows framed two breathtaking sweeps of the river. There was a fairytale touch to the whole thing. But I am a hard nut. I looked under the bed, inside the wardrobe and behind the curtains.

As we checked out the next day, the manager came running out of his cabin.

'Don't take their money,' he told the cashier, 'Or I'll lose my job!'

It turned out that, though Dad was careful to hide our whereabouts from our relatives, he could not resist spilling the beans to his old friend. So Vishnubhai generously gifted Joe and I two views of the gorgeous Mandovi.

Fatima M. Noronha

Just on Time

I reached the VIP cottage, my waiting room, almost panting. And not a minute too soon for just then I glimpsed a swift and sleek convoy of twenty cars slowly turn into the drive. It was a pleasant winter afternoon and the sun rays bounced happily from the shining exterior of the cars, lending them an added sparkle.

Yes, the baraat had arrived. Absolutely on time. And as the cars came to a graceful halt, the descending guests were welcomed by the beating of drums followed by a magical eruption of music. Rose petals floated in the air, thrown by what seemed like a thousand hands and everyone was smiling and hugging. I so wanted to run all the way back to the entrance and join in the unfolding scenes of joyous excitement. But I didn't. My heart was beating very fast now as I gazed into the colourful gathering of friends and family. The youngsters were singing *le jayenge le jayenge dilwale dulhania le jayenge* with gay abandon and in their midst, right in the epicentre of all the activity, I spotted the love of my life, the groom.

Then I saw my mother welcoming him with tilak and aarti and my eyes began to mist with emotion. I can never forget that beautiful moment. And I can never forget that day. Though everything very nearly did not pan off that perfectly... The first hint of trouble came in the morning. The pandit who had to do the morning puja where we were staying disappeared for some other ceremony and it was some time before papa could track him down. That led to a delay of about three hours and required a quick change of appointment with the beautician. But when the beautician overshot her time by two hours, alarm bells were set off all around. Twenty minutes to go before the arrival of the baraat and we (my mother, sister and I) were still at the salon. We were also twenty minutes away from the marriage venue. My to-be in laws and my parents were always close friends and I thought it would be wonderful that we'd all arrive together — the baraat and the bride. My mother was not particularly delighted by the idea. What is the worry, one might ask. Which Indian wedding ever takes place on time? Doesn't the baraat invariably arrive two to six hours late? Going by that standard, I was at least two hours before schedule. But no, that was not going to be the case today and we all knew it.

The thing is, it was a fauji wedding. My father and father-in-law are army officers. Not just that, our grandfathers, our uncles, our brothers, our friends, in short the entire guest list was an assortment of army officers and their families! They would most certainly be on time. We got out of the parlour, and saw papa and my younger brother drive in. It amused me to think that everything was ready at the marriage venue but for a small detail... The bride and her family were missing! 'Hop in,' said papa, dismissing the taxi we had called for and in an instant we were off at breakneck speed. We were late but it didn't matter to me. I was getting married to my sweetheart today and nothing could burst that happy bubble. But mom and papa were tense. And as papa hit the accelerator, I got the most thrilling car ride of my life. Mom was busy with her prayer chants, papa was driving madly through traffic, my brother and sister were not really certain what all the fuss was about and I busied myself singing SRK songs in my mind.

Mom's prayers were powerful. We reached the venue without a hitch and there was still a minute to go. Obviously, the Gods were watching over us. Papa parked the car and all the ladki waale cheered loudly and happily when they saw me arrive. It all made the bright winter afternoon so much prettier. In seconds, someone handed the aarti plate to my mother. My father, brother and uncles took position at the entrance, gorgeous welcoming garlands in hand; some cousins volunteered to chaperone me to my waiting room. I confidently told everyone I'd be fine. I whispered a quick 'I love you' to my parents and family and then... I ran. Yes, in full bridal wear, straight ahead through the entrance gate, wedding venue, the lawns, the chairs, right past the pandaal, through the passage and into the VIP cottage booked for me to wait. Breathless and ecstatic I turned back to look... And that's when I saw the gorgeous convoy arrive. It must have been filmy — what with a speeding car, music, drums, flying rose petals and my Kajol from *DDLJ* moment where I got to run full speed in bridal wear.

Today when I look back, I am happy that we made it that day. My in-laws, being the wonderful people that they are, would not have made anything of a two-minute delay. In fact, as they told me later, they would have really enjoyed surprising the bride and her family by welcoming 'us' with garlands and music had they got the opportunity to do so! But in spite of that, I am happy that we did reach on time and that my parents were not embarrassed, even if it would have been in only their own eyes.

Aarti K. Pathak

Legally-Wedded

I got married again, but to the same man. No, I am not addicted to marriage, but we wanted to be fair to each other and experience both cultures, Indian and Australian. I think they make good memories too.

Last year on June 16, I tied the knot and as with all things Indian, the wedding was long, elaborate and had lots of people. We chose Iskon temple as the elders in my family are very closely connected to it, and because I found it cheap. All I did was visit the temple twice to book and make arrangements. The temple gave us a pandit who was available on his mobile phone. And Pandit Kamlesh obliged when I requested for an English transcription of the vows or prayers, and to make the ceremony short and simple.

My family was arriving a few days ahead of the marriage, just as the groom was. Being the independent girl who had independently chosen her spouse, I was at the helm of things. I think I managed fine. The temple venue looked resplendent in yellow and gold on the wedding day. When I arrived, wearing a simple red Banarasi saree, two gold bangles, my mother's earrings and necklace gifted by my sister, Pandit Kamlesh asked me, 'Dulhan kaha hain?' (Where is the bride?). I smiled, he apologised. Then I reminded him that we enter the temple for the jaimala or exchange of garlands as he had suggested. 'Of course,' he said and led us all. That was when my cell phone was seized because I was beginning to look like a CEO dulhan.

After the jaimala, we came to the venue outside (no wedding is held inside the temple) and we sat down for the rituals and walked around the fire. My friend Boni, who had specially flown from Chennai, commented it was the most relaxed marriage she had ever attended. I know what she meant. All my life I have attended weddings where the atmosphere is sombre, the bride is crying or serious and she cannot afford to laugh for fear of being labelled shameless. On the contrary, I was busy explaining to my non-plussed husband what he had to do and that the sindoor was for him to apply on me and not ask whose turn it was to apply. My father and the husband were caught in a communication gap, each trying desperately to understand the other's accent and failing miserably.

Soon, as the rituals progressed, Pandit Kamlesh and his accomplice threw my composure out of gear. Contrary to the Rs 1,200 fees, they started asking us to dole out hundreds of rupees for each prayer — a 500 rupee note with one banana, a hundred rupee note with one coconut, another hundred for another fruit. I thought this was insane, he was duping us right under our nose. 'Nahi Panditji, aisa nahi chalega (this will not work),' I found myself telling them. We were caught haggling like we were in the middle of a vegetable market amid all the cameras and an annoying TV crew that followed us. I wasn't a celebrity but I was marrying an Australian when Indians were at the receiving end of alleged racist attacks Down Under. So we were a subject of interest. Finally, my friend Geeta intervened and we settled for an amount and proceeded with the ritual.

Then came the turn for vows to be exchanged. A white piece of paper was taken out by the pandits. It was hard not to control the laughter as the men took turns to read out in English what a husband and a wife are supposed to do for the rest of their married life. I don't remember all of it but I do remember one which said of the bride that 'you will take permission from your husband to go out'. I didn't know whether to run or stay put. I was just glad it got over in one-and-a-half hours of putting up with a load of crap and pandits who just recited mantras after mantras after learning them by heart and sucking money out of the occasion while munching pouches of Pan Parag in front of the holy fire.

After the ceremony, we headed off to the temple dining hall for our vegetarian fare for all my friends and neighbours we had invited. The next day, we threw a party for all my friends and that was an evening to remember. I sang, I danced, I drank. Someone said it was a first to see a bride enjoy her own wedding so much. I wondered who, if not me, was to feel the happiest. And what was wrong in enjoying my own wedding! Alas, I did not sit on a chair, demure and weepy-faced.

A year later, I was at the Old Registry building at Spring Street, Melbourne. Amid a close group of ten-twelve friends, I found myself wearing a simple black dress and not worrying that I had no showy jewellery on me. I entered one of the small rooms we had booked and the celebrant took us into a room and rehearsed the ceremony with us. After that, she asked us our choice of music. The minute everyone was seated, she played Bach and asked us whether we were both legally free to marry. Then she made us repeat simple, sweet vows in a silent room and we sealed our marriage with a kiss and exchange of rings and signing of our wedding certificate. It was over in half-an-hour. Legally wedded, we headed for coffee and yumcha. In the evening, amid friends we called it a day with champagne and wine toast, laughter and banter.

I enjoyed both the marriages but I realised Australia is a country that gives you choices. A choice to remain simple, a choice to pick your spouse, a choice to live life by your own dictum.

Laisram Indira

Our Marriage

We were in a special bond of love. We wanted to get married. But life was not as easy as it should have been.

I came from a Maharashtrian family. Ganesh came from a GSB, South Indian family. He was TDH (Tall, Dark and Handsome), just like I had dreamt of my prince charming after reading Mills and Boons during my teenage years. We met in our first job. The bell rang in my heart whenever I saw him. I wondered where I had seen him. I kept questioning him whether he had seen me anywhere. The answer was always a 'No'. We became friends, he proposed, I accepted. The companionship was so enjoyable that we decided to take a step further and convert the relationship into marriage.

After a year-and-a-half, we decided to get married. Due to caste differences, we expected opposition from his family. We wanted to secure our future by buying a flat and saved towards it. As expected, though my parents were very happy with the groom, his parents objected and my gutsy hero conveniently refused to go ahead with the marriage.

I was devastated, heartbroken. My ego did not allow me to speak to him for two whole months. The entire office, which knew of our love story and supported us, understood we had broken up. Many friends expressed their regret that it had not worked out.

We kept getting updates about each other from common friends, and I got to know that he too was going through a difficult time.

Knowing that he still cared, I called him on his cell and asked him to come out of the office, to speak for a few minutes. Seeing him, I couldn't hold back my tears and I cried in his arms. I asked, 'Will you marry me?'

'Yes,' was the answer.

But how? All our investments were in the newly purchased flat and we did not have any savings to get married. So we decided to keep the relationship going and then decide about marriage later on.

In the meantime, my mom had started searching for a groom for me. As I was committed again, I told her to stop her search. She got the hint and informed my dad, who was angry with Ganesh for making me go through hell. He met Ganesh's dad in his office and there was a heated argument between the two. The bomb exploded in his house once again.

This time, we had to take a drastic step. Ganesh was being pressurised to leave me, but we were very firm. There was no looking back.

One evening, when we were sitting in a restaurant with friends for evening snacks, Ganesh announced, 'We both are together again. Things are not good in our families. We would be getting married in a week's time. For this, we want your support.' It was music to my ears. I couldn't believe him saying this so confidently.

Ganesh stayed in our new flat alone due to pressures from family. On 11 March 2004, a Thursday, I got a call from him while I was reaching office, 'Where are you? I have decided that we are getting married tomorrow. Let's go and stay in our flat tonight and tomorrow we shall go to court and get married.'

I was speechless, and didn't know how to react. It was like a dream coming true, though not in a way that I would have liked. I said, 'Don't you think you are giving me a very short notice?' His reply was simple, 'Yes, maybe. But I love you and want to get married to you as early as possible. Before family pressures and other circumstances go against us, let's tie the knot.' There was no reason for me to say no. I agreed. But I was not fine with the idea of staying in the flat overnight before marriage. I told him I would go home and come properly dressed the next day, for marriage.

When I reached office, I could see friends making the preparations for the wedding. I felt like a princess. Even though the preparations were on a small scale, the amount of emotions and love that our friends showed was just amazing. I was on top of the world. I knew that in the next twenty-four hours, I would be married.

The next day, I borrowed a dress on false pretext, took the ration card as proof of residence and started for office. In one corner of my heart, I was scared, hoping that I wasn't taking a wrong step, and the other corner of my heart was secretly smiling for my dream coming true.

We got married in total filmy style with pheras and rituals. Ganesh tied the mangalsutra around my neck, which he had purchased for me long time back. I was the happiest person on earth. I had married the love of my life. I was his 'Bride'.

With a mere gas connection in the house, we started our life, converting it into our home. With time, both the families happily accepted us and now, we too are part of their happy and sad times.

I then realised that I used to see my prince charming in my dreams. Hence I always found Ganesh's face so familiar that I asked him if we had met earlier. I started believing in the statement 'Marriages are made in heaven'.

Today, after being happily married for more than six years, with a cute three-year-old daughter, we remember our marriage date of 12 March 2004 and smile over it. Memories of that day are so fresh in our minds that it feels like we were married just yesterday. The one difference is that, we were thinner at that time!

Komal Kudva

The Perfect Wedding

A wedding is a prime example of the saying 'Man proposes, God disposes'! I had been told by countless brides that nothing happens according to plan, but I too made the mistake of thinking that I'm different. *My* wedding would be perfect!

So, the date was fixed. I decided to quit my job so I could concentrate on getting married. I was doing everything I was supposed to, basking in the love showered by my parents, swiping dad's credit card as if there were no tomorrow and trying to lose weight and regain my glow all at the same time. Like all other weddings, mine had its share of chaos: the tailor didn't give me my blouses till three days before the wedding; I fought with the folks; the DJ was yet to be finalised — in short, I was becoming Bridezilla!!!

One of the reasons I was so excited about my wedding was that it gave me a guilt-free pass to do as much shopping as I wanted. Right from the sarees and churidars to accessories for them and bags and shoes, the list just went on. Also, this is the time when you get pampered the most, so I took ample advantage of it. I meticulously worked on my looks for D-Day, going for trials with the tailor, the make-up lady and discussing it with my family. But being the typical Indian family, even a harmless question such as 'how should I do my hair?' spiralled into hour-long debates which never led to anything conclusive. On the day of the wedding, as I walked out on the stage accompanied by Amma and Appa, all the efforts were worth it when my fiancé looked at me and said, 'You look stunning.'

I have always been a people's person. One of those who'd be open to painting the town red with friends at 2 a.m. simply because aren't friends the family we choose? I have been blessed with great friends all my life. What I didn't expect was that due to various circumstances and a bad stroke of luck, most of my closest friends wouldn't make it for my wedding. I'd expected all of them to come, and until the last minute, didn't know the final status of whether they would or not. Being the hopeless optimist, I'd hoped they would make it. The day before D-Day, when I finally came to know about the people who weren't coming, I couldn't take it anymore. I broke down, thinking of all that I'd done for my friends and how they didn't come for my most important day. It's a difficult pill to swallow, knowing that you've given more than you finally got in return.

I must admit I was very bitter. What I failed to see was this. I was marrying the man of my choice who loved me to bits. Both our families were not just okay about it (as is mostly the case in India) but accepted each other with open arms. I was surrounded by my whole family who had come down only to share my happiness. I was having the marriage of my dreams right in front of my eyes and when I realised this, I started enjoying my wedding.

One of those recurrent questions people always ask when you talk wedding is, 'Are you ready to get married?' Such questions are mostly asked by those who are yet to tie the knot. I never knew how to answer this question. Was this a way to freak me out? If yes, then it totally worked! And this only helped muddle my head even further! Suddenly I started thinking, maybe I'm too young to get married… I'm not wife material… Oh no, here goes freedom… What the hell am I doing?! Fortunately, my fiancé was freaking out too, so we'd share our stories and that helped abate some of the tension.

And yes, to answer that question, I didn't know if I was ready for marriage up until the moment when it actually happened. As I sat on my father's lap, looking up into my husband's eyes as he tied the knot that sanctified our wedding, tears of joy welled up. At that moment, I knew I'd had my perfect wedding!

Ranjani Rengarajan

Second-time Bride

Ravi saw Nitya's picture in his neighbourhood friend's sports day album when he was a teenager. He was at once smitten with the fair and petite Nitya wearing a smile and two plaits but was clueless as to how to get in touch with her. Those were the pre-Facebook times (in the Eighties) when there used to be one big black or red telephone in the entire household and mobile phones were unheard of. In the absence of adequate resources and as time passed, Ravi's crush became blurred in his mind. A decade later, Ravi met a girl while socialising with some common friends. He took an instant liking to her and asked her for an evening out. She agreed and more dates followed, with leisurely hours spent at Ravi's bachelor pad and long drives in Lutyen's Delhi. Two passionate years later, Ravi proposed to her, she didn't agree immediately, but couldn't stick to her 'no commitment' stand for more than one year. Her parents were clearly opposed to the match and asked Nitya, yes she was the same Nitya whom Ravi had liked and longed for in his teenage, to break off with Ravi.

Nitya lied to her family that she had given up on Ravi. She

hadn't. On the contrary, they were planning to get married secretly and were saving money for their wedding. Back then, Ravi was working in a private firm and Nitya was pursuing her higher studies. They were scared of the families' disapproval but were determined to spend life with each other. One fine day, they decided to tie the knot and began preparations for their marriage. Soon, shopping commenced at Lajpat Nagar (a popular marketplace in south Delhi); a heavily embroidered red lehenga and tacky artificial jewellery for Nitya and a cheap suit for Ravi, and they were set to become man and wife. No month-long shopping and detailed planning, just one trip to the market and a temple to organise the wedding.

The D-Day arrived and Nitya was both nervous and excited. She had always wanted an elaborate wedding with all the rituals and family members at her side, mehendi, haldi and female relatives fussing over her. But that was obviously not to be. Nitya had made a quick trip a day before the marriage to a beauty parlour with a friend to get the mehendi done and had given the lehenga for ironing to the dhobi herself. The next day, her wedding day, she got up, took a generous amount of time showering and now was the time for the soon-to-be bride to be bedecked in her bridal finery. Her friends came and helped her dress up and apply make-up, complete with bright red lipstick and jasmine flowers. Soon Ravi came to pick her up and along with a small group of excited friends who were obviously thrilled with the adventurous nature of the marriage a la Bollywood style, they were on way to the temple.

The ceremony didn't take long to start, considering that there was precious little to do on the sunny winter morning with a handful of guests and a small hawan kund. The pandit, a comic figure, quickly made them exchange garlands and started reciting the mantras for the pheras. When Nitya asked the meaning of a particular Sanskrit verse, the pandit switched to colloquial Hindi interspersed with jokes and topical examples of marriage in recent times with much glee. In a span of two hours, Nitya and Ravi were husband and wife. Post sweets and a frugal lunch, the newly wedded couple reached their home, Nitya's first marital home. They spent the rest of the day discussing how to break the news of their wedding to their families. A cousin helped do the deed and Nitya's family was calling her next morning to confirm if what they had heard was true. Once Nitya confirmed the news, her father wished her congratulations and cried and her mom asked them not to worry about anything and be calm. 'So you got married, congrats,' said her dad. Nitya wasn't sure if it was pure unconditional parental blessing or had a fair sprinkling of sarcasm. It was nevertheless an anti-climax. Nitya had expected her parents to scream and shout at her but what followed were just tears and assurances.

Nitya's family met Ravi's family and after some usual ego clashes, they decided on a date for their 'second marriage' to make it official and respectable. The lovebirds were simply informed about the new development and asked to book their tickets for their home town a week prior to the official wedding (they had a common hometown). It doesn't take great imagination to know that the newly-wedded couple was looking forward to the fresh round of ceremonies for their marriage with a sense of relief and some trepidation too. Well, they were to face their families for the first time since they had tied the knotty knot. 'How do you think our families will react after seeing us,' Nitya asked Ravi. 'Will be good fun seeing different kinds of reactions,' was all Ravi said.

In time for their second marriage, Nitya and Ravi reached their hometown and bade each other temporary farewell on the railway station, to go to their respective homes. The rituals prior to the wedding were not a long drawn affair, more of a quick thing, a smattering of haldi here, a prayer there. Now the second D-Dday arrived and Nitya got a chance to be a bride once again. This time, the bridal jewellery was real and more real was the presence of people who mattered for the bride. She was again prettified for the wedding ceremony, attended to by relatives and very few friends from both sides. But this time the differences from the 'first marriage' were apparent. The function was in a hotel, not a temple and Ravi arrived with full fanfare dressed in a formal suit with all the trappings of a bridegroom, in a rose-decked car and with a full baraat. The garlands were again exchanged, mantras recited again and the traditional Hindu wedding indispensable ingredient sindoor smeared once again in Nitya's hair parting. The second time bride was on her way to her second marital home, right after the wedding and this time she did feel like a coy bride in the brand new environs of her husband's home, with endless rounds of sacraments and revelry.

Pallavi Shankar

Taking the Cake

Jay and Asha had a 'fruitful' day, tasting cakes. The woman at the bakery had been amazingly helpful. She drew up some gorgeous sketches of cakes in keeping with their theme. But the price tag put a slight downer on their mood.

'Do we really need a cake?' Jay asked Asha.

'Of course! Have you attended any wedding reception that didn't have a cake?' For Asha, not having a cake was unthinkable.

'How many times have you eaten cake at a reception, especially when there's ice cream, gulab jamuns, a chocolate fountain and rasogullas?'

'But it's so pretty. It will make the wedding pictures even lovelier!' Asha replied.

'I just don't know if getting some pictures is worth the price tag...'

Asha's face dropped. Jay thought for a while and then suggested, 'Let's reason out why people have cakes at their wedding and then decide whether we want one or not.'

Asha reluctantly agreed. They concluded on two explanations.

1) Cutting the cake was symbolic of being the first task that the couple does together.

2) Feeding each other cake represented the idea of a couple providing for each other in their marriage.

Asha got thinking. They had so many other beautiful things in their wedding that would provide for great pictures. Why did they need a cake for it?

After a lot of deliberation, Asha found her answer. She and Jay were both lovers of nature. Planting a tree would be the first task they would do together as a couple.

The tree would be something they could watch grow over the years. It would stand as a permanent reminder of their special day. The tree symbolised generosity and solidarity, two qualities essential to keep a marriage working. While a cake disappeared in minutes, the tree would stay with them forever!

This summer the tree turned three.

Heena Patel

The Happiest Day of My Life

The more I think about the happiest day of my life, the sadder I get. Great shift in paradigm there.

Blushing and very young, not yet twenty-two, as I sat on that beautifully decorated dais, the heady smell of roses and marigold engulfed my mind and body. It was the first wedding in my family and my dad had not left any stone unturned. The shamiana was huge, flower decorations all around, the smell of the lavish dinner wafting in the air. The photographer was taking his job very seriously, asking me to pose, look in different directions and clicking away from every conceivable angle. I basked in all my bridal glory, happily obliging the photographer's requests.

Soon it was time to take pictures with the family and my husband's very large extended family came up one after the other and surrounded us gleefully, little children finding place to sit between my husband and I. The photographer was delighted. My parents were called next. I saw them approaching the dais. They weren't smiling; in fact they looked sad to me. Well, it was the day their daughter would leave them to be a part of her new family. Parents of a bride are bound to feel sad and emotional even through all their happiness and excitement.

But as they came nearer, my heart sank. My usually dapper dad was looking oddly dishevelled, to say the least. He was not wearing his blazer anymore and his tie looked clumsily knotted. His eyes were red and hair uncombed and he somehow shuffled up the dais. I pretended not to have noticed. He came and sat on the arm of my elaborate throne-like chair, and put one arm around my shoulder lovingly. I turned away. The photographer asked me to look up and smile. I did not. I did not smile in any of those pictures, didn't even look up, much to the photographer's disdain.

Tears clouded my vision and anger filled my thoughts. I wanted to let go of all my bridal timidity and confront my father. 'Why? How could he do this to me? It's the day of my wedding, the happiest day of my life. Could he not have avoided getting drunk today, just this one day? Could he not resist the temptation for the sake of his child?'

The photo session on the stage ended. Guests were already eating dinner, laughing, talking; all eyes seemed to be on me. I didn't bother to smile... I frowned, almost cried with anger. The pheras and kanyadaan were more private rituals with only close family members in attendance.

It was way past midnight and my dad just about managed to sit through the puja... My mother didn't look happy either. I wanted to talk to her... She kept avoiding my questioning glances. After all the rituals ended, I was taken into a room where I could rest for a while. My mum and two sisters came and hugged me. I looked at my mum and she cried.

All she kept saying was, 'Be a good girl in your new home, a good daughter to them just as you've been to us.' I was crying too, but I had to ask her now ... 'Why did papa have to drink today?' was all I could manage to say in between all the sobbing. She looked at me sadly and said, 'He hasn't had a drop of it since the last four days when the ceremonies began; in fact, he has been fasting all day today. He's been so anxious with all the things happening around and not many hands to help him with the work. He knew he had a lot to do, so he popped in a couple of strong pain killers to kill his arthritis pain and that possibly must've triggered the seizure-like attack when he did the little jig with the boisterous baraatis.'

I stared at my mom in disbelief. 'What are you talking about?' I asked.

'Oh baby, we didn't want you upset, it's your big day today, so papa asked us not to let you know. We called in a doctor to see him, he was better after a while and wanted to continue with all the rituals just as planned.'

'Where is he now?' I asked.

'He must be getting on with the bidaai rituals. He has to be there to thank everyone for coming.'

'I want to see him now,' I said.

My brother walked in to say it was time for me to leave; my hubby's family was waiting for me. I came out, guilty of misjudging my father, for not having had the faith in him. How could I have got so caught up with my happiness that I failed to see that my dad was unwell? I went to him, hugged him tight and cried. And he was crying too, all the while saying, 'Be good, Beans,' (his pet name for me).

I was escorted into the bedecked car. My brother and cousins gave the car a little push, suggestive of lifting the doli of the olden times... The car moved slowly. I didn't want to leave my father then.

I leaned out of the car window and said, 'Sorry papa, I love you!'

Vandana Vij

The Importance of A Wedding 'Ceremony'

I pride myself on being a very well educated, extensively travelled and hence ultimately a modern, forward-thinking person. Having lived in Australia for six years, the UK for two and the US for one, when it came to my marriage, conventional Indian notions did not seem applicable. I will be getting married at the end of this year in December! I fell in love with my fiancé, who had been a close friend for years, and we decided to get married as soon as we entered a relationship.

Luckily for me, he was equally forward thinking and we found that as the wedding planning drew close, we largely wanted the same things for our wedding. With his father in the Indian Foreign Service, Arunabh has grown up in seven countries, having changed schools nine times throughout his learning years. This, of course, makes him a global citizen with little need for long elaborate wedding celebrations, which are so characteristic of Indian weddings.

Both Arunabh and I were initially very happy to have a civil ceremony, which entailed a mere signature in the presence of the wedding registrar. We decided to get married under the Special Marriages Act, which is a legal provision for couples of different communities in India.

Our parents also accepted our request to have a very simple, low-key wedding affair with a registration and a reception if they deemed necessary. As time went by, we were required to submit a 'notice' for approval with the registrar, which had to be served ninety days before the wedding date. Arunabh and I got all the necessary documents ready and marched in to the government office where these needed to be submitted.

After an hour-long wait in the hot and musty dilapidated room of the wedding registrar, we were called. Although we had followed the list of documents required, it took us one hour of negotiations with the inflexible government authorities to even get them to have a look at our documents. While we were waiting, I saw young couples lined up waiting to put down that signature that would legally declare them 'married'.

As that point I realised that the memory of my wedding would be waiting in a long queue in this dusty old office only to be met by a grumpy government official who would make it an elaborate task just to wed us. I thought to myself, 'Is this what I want for my wedding?' It jolted me and I handed in our notice and left that office as fast as my feet would take me.

When I walked out of the office, I started thinking of the importance of a wedding 'ceremony' for the bride and the groom. The forty-five-minute-long ceremony may be words that you don't understand or prayers that a priest chants, but it instils a feeling of finality. So even though a ceremony may largely be a public proclamation, it also has a very private impact on the couple.

As it stands for me now, even though I believed differently for all these years, I do not wish to have the most important step of my life solemnised with a mere signature. I do not want our marriage to feel like a contract, or that I am making a business transaction and all I need to do is sign on the bottom line. I wish to have the echo of prayers around us, I wish to have a memory of sitting in front of a priest with my husband-to-be and feel the magnitude of the most important decision of our lives — our marriage to each other.

We have just booked a priest who will now conduct a ceremony in a wonderful garden setting. A short, sweet, simple ceremony amidst our close family and friends. We have also requested him to speak in English on marriage, so we can understand the implications of this next step of ours together. Yes, it will serve as a social proclamation, but more importantly, it will signify a time of reflection, contemplation and acceptance of each other as we sit through the rituals.

Shanaya Mody

While the Family Thought
She Was in College

As she sat in a rickety autorickshaw in the sweltering summer heat, with a man who she had met a couple of hours ago, Simran wondered what she was doing. Was she actually being hurled towards a court house to get married? Was she going to be a bride in these faded jeans and pink tee? After twenty-five years of dreaming of a fairy tale wedding...

Simran met Bijoy online six months ago. While she was ensconced in her lovely family home in Vancouver, he was in PG digs with another struggling actor in Mumbai. It was love at first byte! Yet, both didn't believe in online romances leading to anything... He continued to have his flings while acting in plays and TV serials. She continued seeing boys who her mom and assorted aunts kept lining up.

Yet, when cupid decides to strike, logic loses all meaning. So pictures were exchanged, webcams bought and soon there was a romance that seemed real and wonderful. Could he move to Canada? Would she like living in Mumbai? Nicknames were given, confiding in friends happened, she got gorgeous bangles in the mail, he found chocolates delivered at his doorstep.

Six months passed by in a daze... A wonderful time where all that mattered was spending every waking moment together, so what if it was only virtual. Till her brother caught on and all hell broke loose. How could she dare to talk to some strange man? He is the one I love and will marry, she declared. She knew very little about him or his family and yet she was sure. Her parents hit her and locked her up at home. She knew she had to do something.

He was distraught in Mumbai as she was never online or answering the phone. He got me, his gal pal, to call the land line and I was told that Simran was in college. Bijon was losing his mind and his friends rallied around him. Simran called one night to tell him that she was running away from home and coming to Mumbai the next day. They had to get married...

There he was at the airport, clutching onto a bouquet of roses, hoping he would recognise his wife-to-be. His friends were waiting at home, hoping things would work out. I was one of them, curious to meet this brave girl who had done something none of us would have the guts to do. He called and the joy leaping out of his voice was touching, like he had topped his board exams! They were going to a coffee shop and he would keep us posted.

Now, we were on tenterhooks, imagining the worst. Why weren't they coming home? Had she developed cold feet? Not liked Bijon? I had told him not to wear those floaters. He called at 5 a.m. and asked us to be at the Bandra court at 8 a.m. with flowers and mithai for the wedding.

We met them and I could clearly see how lost and confused Simran looked. In love and happy, but lost... Amidst much cheering and laughter, they signed a register and got married. A celebratory lunch followed and that's where she and I bonded. I could get it when she said she didn't feel married, with tears threatening to spill over any moment. She asked for help.

That's what friends are for. My mom was let into the secret and the party shifted to my place. A dholak and mehendiwali were organised. A designer friend came and started organising her outfit. Another pal made bookings in the gurdwara. It was the most lovely mehendi and sangeet. All of us dressed up. Simran wore a new outfit and the gold jhumkas Bijon rushed out and got her. My elder brother made her wear the chooda and we all sang through the night.

The next morning, the pheras happened in the gurdwara and my parents did the kanyadaan. She called her parents in Vancouver and mother and daughter sobbed on the phone. She insisted on coming back to my house from where the bidaai happened and when she finally did enter Bijon's small little home, she was beaming... And looked every inch the glowing bride.

Shifa Maitra

Without Approval

I wept copious tears at the registrar's office. No creamy silks for me, I was dressed in a new lungi (the fashion before bell-bottoms came in) and blouse bought off Colaba Causeway. My mangalsutra was strung in thread, only the locket was made of gold. Glass bangles, a stick-on bindi, a veni in my hair, and a new pair of chappals. That was my trousseau. My bag contained a few clothes, some money I'd withdrawn from my meagre account and a photograph of my family. I was not to see them for many years. They were angry, they were hurt. Lucky me, they admitted that they could make mistakes, and finally we were welcomed into the fold again. But this is the story of me as a bride.

K and I were college mates, we fell in love, and as was not uncommon in the Sixties, our parents disapproved. They disapproved of many things: films, film songs, and informal mixing of boys and girls. They disapproved of my choice of mate; first of the romance itself. Their reputation was at stake when their girl was seen with a boy. However, this was the era of liberation, higher education, careers for women and I wasn't going to blindly obey norms and rigid social or familial rules. We women of the Sixties were free to think, earn and decide for ourselves. Caste and language weren't barriers, and we were confident enough to go ahead and realise our dreams.

Easier said than done. My parents employed someone to be my chaperone. This ayah was a stern woman, extremely loyal to my parents and very conservative. Ducking her watch was a daily creative exercise. I bunked practicals, invented laboratory 'duties', found secret means of escape at lunch-break, and we played this game of catch-me-if-you-can for a couple of months. Then I was openly defiant. All the yelling and scolding at home had made me adamant. From my grandmother down to the toddler in the upstairs flat told me to stop-stop-stop this 'nonsense'.

In contrast, the man I was in love with, K, was so much more in control, so much more forgiving of my parents' behaviour, so much more mature. He wasn't concerned about what relatives or neighbours would say and, over a period of time, neither was I. So after a while, we simply ignored the ayah and went where we liked without hiding behind parked cars or climbing over compound walls. Our friends, of course, were with us. Many of them were in the same predicament, facing opposition at home at their choice of life-partners. Quite a few eventually gave in to parental pressure. We didn't. It was a time when anything that we did was frowned upon: rock 'n' roll music, jam sessions, comics, smoking, drinking, eating out at corner stalls, talking slang and mingling with the other gender. Oh yes, singing Beatles' songs and wearing faded jeans, too. Very few did drugs, but our parents were paranoid. If a boy grew his hair and tied it into a ponytail, he was definitely 'out'. If a girl wore worn and fraying jeans and took part in morchas (common in those days, there was always a cause to fight for), she was treading away from the straight and narrow. Naturally, I was a big let-down for them. Heartbreak, sorrow at having such a 'bad' offspring was their problem. The guilt-trip was mine.

Much stealth and slyness was involved in booking the date at the Marriage Registrar's office. For four weeks leading up to the event, I smuggled out my personal belongings. Some things were hidden in friends' homes, some taken to K's parents' house but without their knowledge. On the morning of my wedding, I walked out of the house — forever — as if I was going to college as usual, with my tiffin in my purse, with spare coins for the commute and mother's 'don't forget to return the library books' ringing in my ears as I stepped out.

All brides must feel nervous. Some, like me, might be terrified, excited, foolish, daring, all at once. I can't describe what I felt, though so many years down the line I can relive the emotion, or emotions. I have done that so, so many times. When I go for weddings even today, I feel like an alien. When I eat at the fancy banquets, I remember the treat K and I gave our dear, dependable friends: chai and samosas. We shared those with the registrar and distributed pedhas. Wearing garlands and with our haversacks on our back, we took the local train to Juhu. Our honeymoon was in a friend's parents' vacant flat.

Those were pre-mobile phone days. My parents were frantic when I didn't return that evening. They phoned my friends, went from house to house asking about me. They were told I was safe, but none revealed my whereabouts. They didn't go to the police. Instead, they got in touch with K's parents, who were surprised, because they didn't know of our marriage either.

Fortunately, my parents-in-law welcomed me with open arms. They were curious at my audacity, but pleased that I could leave my own folks for their son. I entered their house on the third day after my unusual wedding. They insisted on a traditional entry. So finally I did wear a colourful attire, got my hair done up nicely, smeared a borrowed lipstick on my lips, and faced a thaali full of lit lamps and rice grains before I entered, barefoot, my future home. No feasting, no glittering lights, no presents. But I was content.

Did I regret this non-celebration? Not in the least. I was a bride. A happy young woman, in love with a fine young man of her choice. Our chemistry matched perfectly. The world didn't matter. Were I to relive my life over again, I'd do exactly what I did... And get pampered by my groom for the rest of my life. Parties and decorations are trivia. What matters to the bride is the future. Mine was, has been, secure, fun-filled and satisfying.

As told to Sheela Jaywant

6

AN ARRANGED MARRIAGE

In all of the wedding cake, hope is the sweetest of plums.

–Douglas William Jerrold

Arranged Love...

After my elder sister got married, it was my turn to settle down. I had issues with the traditional Indian way of finding an alliance. A girl walks in to a room full of strange people balancing a tray with tea and snacks in her hands. I didn't want to be put through such a grind.

In Indian Muslim families, it was the norm to dress more traditionally as you approach marriageable age. My younger sister was already doing that. But I was fond of my jeans and skirts. I went ahead and cut my hair very short too. My logic being that any man who would agree to marry me would have to be broad minded enough to accept all this.

Same rebel streaks made me go for a job interview at a local travel agency even though I was a trained computer teacher. The manager was from Kolkata. He kept reassuring me that the job was mine to take. I came back home thinking he must be a creep.

I got the job and came to know from the manager that not only were my qualifications right for the post, I was also 'suitable' for one of his friends. His friend, a well-educated interior designer, was looking for a smart educated girl from a decent Muslim family. However, he was not comfortable meeting a girl in the traditional set up. His reasons being the girl would be conscious and so would he. Wow, here was a man who matched my mindset.

I was always receptive to the idea of meeting an alliance outside my home. All I prayed was for him not to be a lungi-clad, paan-chewing conservative Muslim fellow.

Soon enough, he came down from Kolkata to our office. I was informed the previous day about his arrival. So the next day, I went to office wearing faded jeans, making sure I did not look made up. Around 11 a.m., in walked this person with the most casual bearings and laziest smile. There was no thunder or rain but I was certainly washed over with a sense of comfort. That feeling was brand new for a girl like me.

He sat with the manager and kept staring at me all through the day. Just before I was to pack up for the day, he came over to my seat to book a return flight ticket for the following evening. I noted his details and booked him on the required flight.

It was then that he asked me out for lunch. Bhubaneswar is a small place and everyone knows everyone. To avoid gossip mongers, I said innocently, 'I would like to go where very few go.' Looking deep into my eyes he asked, 'Are you reading my mind? I want to take you where no one goes too.' In spite of myself, I blushed pink.

We went to Hotel Kenil Worth for lunch. We had a fun and easy time. I told him up front, 'I am anti dowry.' He added, 'I am anti everything you are anti.' As an anti-climax, I messed up his flight timing! He called me from the airport to inform me of the same. He beamed, 'I am happy to get an excuse to talk to you again.'

His friend went to the airport to put him on the right plane. He must be the only client in the history of travel agencies who did not bicker over his ticket mix up.

After two months, our nikah took place. We have been happily married for the last fifteen years. Oh yes, I still wear jeans and skirts. But I have longer hair on his request.

Ghazala S. Hossain

Chemistry

I was all of twenty-two when the battle royale began at home. With both my brothers married, I was the only 'responsibility' my parents had. With my dad due for retirement, the pressure to complete this duty at the earliest must have been double. And so, like in everything else, my mother came to me confidently with a proposal, probably sure that I would simply look down shyly and nod filmy style. So when I said 'No, I am not interested', it threw the spanners in their plans. It was a good proposal, even I knew that, but I was averse to marriage, having seen too many marriages that didn't look happy to me. (I didn't ask the people concerned their opinion of their marriage, of course, but I couldn't see it as being happy.) And then, I had a long list of things I wanted from life — work, dance, social work and just plain fun. Fun and marriage seemed like oxymorons.

But if I expected my otherwise liberal parents to be content with my 'I don't want to marry' as a reason enough, it didn't work. My mother was after me, finally using the 'let's go to a psychiatrist' phrase as her ace card. And, sigh, it worked. So, the boy came and I 'saw' him. We didn't talk to each other, but his sister did. I was very open with her and told her family was my last priority… So we didn't see them after that meeting.

Boy two at twenty-three, boy three at twenty-four, boy four at twenty-five… One a year seemed like a good average, keeping peace in the family. My parents were happy to scan and filter, I was happy to meet and let them know I was not interested in gentle terms. Boys were happy not getting back at all. So no one could blame anyone else.

Thus continued my happy life, till my mother told me about this family that was waiting to see me as a common friend had recommended me to them. By now, I was experienced in handling the 'girl seeing' occasions and had no pressures at all about how this will go. So when the boy and his parents came in, I was my 'hostess' best, polite and warm. 'Not bad looking,' I thought of the boy. 'Let's see how good he is when he opens his mouth.'

Ahem… He was good. Clear, lucid, good language and no hemming and hawing. His parents (incidentally, this was the first time in all the four years that I was in a formal set-up with both sets of parents present, me in a sari, and 'demurely' waiting to be called out) and my parents had common interest in music, both had lived in different parts of the North all their working life and so could compare different cultures, and it became a nice social visit.

Then we were asked to go in and speak to each other to get to know each other. And the forty-five minutes flew! When his father called him out, he joked, 'Will you finish all you have to tell about yourself right now?'

It was really strange, what I felt then. He grinned as he

left the room, and I laughed happily. Since I had several male colleagues and was quite friendly with all of them, in my previous 'dekko'meetings, I had wondered what cut the colleagues from the prospective grooms? Why should I say 'yes' to one man, and not to another?

But with this man, I felt as if I had been talking to someone whom I had known for ages. It was an instant connect and there was not a minute when we didn't have something to say to each other.

They left immediately after. My brother, who stepped in just a few minutes before they were leaving, told my mother, 'They seem like a good family. If Mee is okay with it, then you should go ahead.'

My mother said, even before I said anything, 'She is.'

She knew from my expression that I had finally found my match, that I wanted to spend my life with him.

And for the first time, I hoped that the groom-to-be felt that way too. I felt apprehensive about what the response would be. Next day was a Saturday, when normally such matters were not discussed. But this unconventional family broke that tradition, and called first thing in the morning to say 'yes' to the proposal. Did anyone need to ask me my opinion? It was written clearly on my face.

And for the first time, I understood terms like 'Instant Chemistry' and 'Love at First Sight'.

In another break from tradition, we met every day till our marriage. When safely married, I asked my father, 'How come you let me go out with him?'

My dad replied, 'You both looked so much in love!'

I am glad that ten years and two children down the line, except after a bad fight, I have not regretted the decision.

And, I continue to work and dance and do my little bit as and when I can for the society.

S. *Meera*

Guns and Roses

The day my mother brought up the subject of my marriage, I enrolled for rifle shooting training. The two were unrelated events.

I had turned twenty-five, which was an alarm for the community matchmakers to take up my cause with a vengeance. An uncle made a truckload of copies of my horoscope to be handed to every Tamilian in town.

I wanted to enjoy my independence for as long as I could. As a journalist, I was passionate about my work and liked the unconventional lifestyle it offered. I did not believe in the 'bliss of domesticity' my parents were trying to sell. But I did not want to upset them and instead, let the match-making circus run its course.

I had no idea what kind of person I wanted to spend my life with, but I knew what I did not want. No geeky looking, number crunching, rice and sambhar eating IT engineer for me. That had wiped out ninety-nine per cent of the candidates my parents had lined up for me. But they had their trump card and my father mentioned Prassanna.

'Is he an IT guy?' I asked.

'Yes, but…'

'From the south?'

'Yes... but it's Bangalore, the most cosmopolitan city...'

I frowned and started to walk away in a huff when suddenly my dad called out, 'By the way, he is a rifle shooter.' I stopped and turned around to make sure I had heard him correctly.

'He is a member of a rifle club, just like you,' added my mother.

'What kind of rifle?' I asked.

'We don't know all that. Why don't you speak to him yourself and find out. His number and e-mail ID are behind the photo,' said dad.

My curiosity got the better of me and I added him on my e-mail ID. I had planned that I would be polite but firm in my conversations with him, and was determined to investigate whether this guy could actually handle a firearm.

It was only after one week that he appeared online. 'Hey, nice to see you online FINALLY!' he typed, his first ever words to me. I was miffed and the all-capitals did not help.

'But I thought it was you who didn't know how chat works,' I replied. There was a weird silence for a few minutes.

'Oh!' he wrote, after what seemed like an eternity. 'Did Ramanathan Raman come to see you?'

'Who in the world is that?'

'My engineering classmate,' he replied. 'Word on the street is that his whirlwind bride hunting trip took him to fifteen cities across the country, including yours. Was he there by any chance?'

'Definitely not.'

'Poor chap. All those rejections messed him up and he resorted to what any desperate man in his situation would do.'

'Oh my God!' my fingers flew over the keyboard. 'Did he commit ... suicide?'

'No! He went to the US, so that he could be called a US-returned engineer.'

A familiar rush of anger began to seep in. 'Is this your idea of a JOKE?'

'Not really. My idea of a joke would be a girl willing to talk to me only because I hold a rifle shooting certificate.'

I grappled for a response. 'Glad you like jokes, but it won't be funny when I challenge you to a duel.'

'You're on, lady,' was all he said.

Our families were appalled but we stuck to our 'guns'. Two months later, Prasanna visited my city for the first time. I stood at the airport expecting the typical pot-bellied geek, but out came a tall, handsome guy with a cool pair of shades resting on his head. As he greeted me with a boyish smile and a sporty handshake, I could swear I heard violins in the background.

He chatted incessantly about nothing in particular but was pretty likeable. For the next few days, I got to know him better but the matter of shooting skills was yet to be settled. On his last day in the city, we decided to get closure on that, although I was totally charmed by him and ready to throw the game away, if necessary.

At the rifle club, we were welcomed by a dilapidated board that said 'Maintenance work in progress. Shooting range closed for a week.' I didn't know if I was relieved or disappointed. Prasanna smiled and produced a letter from his pocket. It was his certificate of shooting. 'Well, I brought this just in case...' he said, looking into my eyes for the first time. I blushed.

I ignored the idea of probing into the fact that the certificate had no official seal and the handwriting looked suspiciously familiar. We were married by the end of the year and decided never to undertake a firearm duel for the rest of our lives. The world would be a safer place that way. That is our story... And people still think arranged marriages are boring!

Archana Mohan

Hooked Amidst the Books

'You're getting married!' my best friend screamed in disbelief. 'How did this come about?' After all, I was only twenty-two and, according to her, I had many more years of freedom ahead of me. Besides I had never shown any inclination to get hitched or to settle down! What was wrong with me? Not that there hadn't been proposals or boys interested in me. It was just that they had all been good friends as I had never seen them in a romantic light...

And suddenly, this young Army Captain appeared out of the blue, sweated his way into my stuffy little library (where I sat, all prim and proper, spectacles on nose and frown firmly in place!). That was how I spent my evenings every day after college, managing our very own little library.

When he walked in, all I noticed were his deep dimples, and then I put them, and him, out of my mind. When he asked, 'Can I be a member here?' I just nodded brusquely, wondering whether he had not read the sign outside which advertised for new members!

He was like the sun that appeared on the horizon every day, and he certainly persevered, as rivulets of perspiration flecked his brow and made him keep mopping his face with a spotless white handkerchief which, I later got to know, was part and parcel of his person, for he never left home without one.

One by one, my family members began sending tentative feelers to me. Grandpa airily remarked, 'Good-looking boy... That Army Captain!' even as my grandmother nudged him to make him stop. According to her, well brought up girls were not supposed to even look at boys! My sisters began smiling at him and my mother quite fell for his deep dimples and his brown eyes! His sister claimed, much later, that she was the one who had arranged the meeting, since she had brought him along when she had come to admit her daughter at my mother's school.

I continued along life's course, quite oblivious to the whole charade being played out around me. The young Captain came to the library, morning and evening, reading his books at a particularly uncanny speed, a fact that did not escape me. Luckily I didn't ask him questions on what he had read. For later on in life, he confessed that he had never read so much and skipped so many pages in order to be able to return the books on time!

Over a fortnight we became friends, and soon began talking about many varied topics, all except romance. He told me that he had caught a glimpse of me even before he had become a member of the library. It was then I noticed his warm brown eyes for the first time as he smiled at me.

And then one day, he suddenly asked, 'Would you like to come to Bhuj with me?' And that was it. There was no formal proposal , just a bald question, but that was enough because I had started feeling very secure with him by then.

That evening, the two families were ecstatic. My sisters doted on their future brother-in-law. My mother insisted that he call her 'Amma' instead of 'Ma'am', as had been his wont. My grandparents could not hide their glee. After all, their eldest grandchild had just got engaged! My old nurse, Parvathy Amma, took the young man aside and said to him sternly, 'Now make sure you look after our little girl, or you'll have me to contend with!'

When his parents came to 'see' me, it was more of a cosy, comfortable get-together as there were no awkward moments, and the two families got along like a house on fire.

My paternal grandmother gave me this nugget of advice, since she knew that I had never ever entered the kitchen before. 'Be careful, child, and don't go anyway near the gas stove!' Good advice, to be sure, but hardly practical for a brand new bride!

The wedding day came and went like a flash. There was the typical temple ceremony followed by a proper public wedding where blessings vied with flash bulbs. The only hitch was when the bridegroom decided to hold his bride's wrong hand, and had to walk the customary three rounds facing backward, a rather uncomfortable process while people in the audience were in splits!

The one image that remains embedded in my mind's eye is the nostalgia on my mother's pensive face, amidst all her smiles, as tears streamed down her cheeks. She was missing Dad dreadfully. Dad who would have been so happy to see his eldest daughter getting married, Dad whose life revolved around his precious family, Dad who suffered an unexpected but massive heart attack and succumbed to it, a final betrayal which was not his fault at all!

And thus began our marital adventure, a start to our life together, a rollercoaster ride which helped us know each other better; a ride with all its ups and downs, magical moments, immature spats, new experiences, wheels under our feet as we traversed through the various postings within the Army, and the birth of our wonderful daughter.

Today, as I look back to that day twenty-six years ago, I know deep within my heart that the decision I took then was one of the best I had ever taken in my life. And of course, I do ensure that my husband keeps out of libraries on his own!

Deepti Menon

How I Met the Nair Boy

I always wanted a love marriage. I mean, which girl doesn't? We all are die hard romantics at heart and want a *filmy* type of love story. While some people get lucky and experience that intense passion before marriage, for the rest of us, it happens *after* marriage.

Like I said, I always wanted a love marriage. Many times I came close to the 'love' part of it but not marriage. The commitment phobia always made its presence felt. But instead of wasting time complaining, I would simply move on.

I no longer trusted my choice of guys, so I let my parents do it for me. Some of you may point fingers at me saying, 'This is the modern age, girl! Who goes for arranged marriages nowadays?' But if you're confused, immature and make the most ridiculous choices in life, just like me, I would advise you to let your parents take the matter in their capable hands.

My parents always left the ultimate decision to me — to reject or accept a guy! I kind of misused this option and rejected a good bunch of guys. Everyone was worried, 'Why isn't she liking any guy?', 'Maybe she has a boyfriend!', 'Next time you see any guy, just ACCEPT him... It will work out in the future.' The last advice hurt me and I wondered if these people actually cared for me!

A day arrived when I actually liked a guy's photograph and profile and decided to meet him. Mr Nair. He entered the house with his friend and was surprised to find me already seated in the living room. All he did was give a shy smile. We avoided looking at each other for a while although I chatted with his friend. Mr Nair confessed to me later that for a moment he felt that I would pick his best friend over him!

We were then left alone to talk for a while. The conversation flowed, like never before. What was supposed to be a ten-minute talk stretched to three hours. Everybody wondered, 'What happened? What are they talking about?' There was tension in the air. Mr Nair decided to miss his train and continue talking to me.

He was easy going, had a childlike laugh and I was able to be myself with him in no time. It just clicked. We both said 'yes' and the family was relieved. So was I!

But if you think I am in love, not really! Love doesn't happen in a couple of days or meetings, it grows over time, and right now, I can feel my golden days of love... Just around the corner!

Dhanya Venugopal

No Mucchad for Me, Please

Everybody knew that Juhi had dreamed about her knight in shining armour as tall, dusky, strongly built, well educated with a good job and most importantly... with no moustache! Absolutely no offending bristles that would inconvenience blossoming love.

My aunt searched heaven and earth to find a suitable match for her only child, but most of the eligible bachelors she came upon had a maximum of two points in common with Juhi's formidable list. One day, a family friend showed her their bachelor son's photograph. One look was enough to bring a smile to her lips. The lad in the picture fitted the bill perfectly. The only concern was his proud moustache!

Aunty conspired to make it work. She gave Juhi a detailed description of the charming young man with no mention of the moustache at all. Juhi consented to meet the boy.

The day arrived when the two families met to unite the young souls. Vikram looked dapper in a suit and impressed everyone, including Juhi. His regal moustache had put her off but was this reason substantial enough to reject a worthwhile proposal?

The next day, Vikram went over to pick up Juhi from her work place. She was thrilled to see him ride a Bullet, which easily qualifies as a worthy cousin of the Harley Davidson. He looked elegant in his check shirt and Woodland shoes but the moustache was still an eyesore.

She reflected on her mother's sage advice that facial hair was indeed one's own farm. One could grow them and similarly, shave them too. Juhi graciously accepted his ride home after a cup of coffee. She warmed up to him during the date and the affectionate couple sped away into the sunset. Falling as an unsuspecting victim to Cupid's arrow, she agreed to the marriage proposal without much ado.

The next day came as a rude shock to Juhi. As Vikram wanted to start things on a clean slate, he wanted to set a few records straight. He confessed that the swanky Bullet he rode had been borrowed from his best friend and that he possessed the ever reliable Vespa scooter. All of a sudden, the thick coarse bristles smug on Vikram's upper lip began to bother Juhi again. She would dream of them piercing deep into her skin leaving ugly sting marks. It was time to hatch a plan before the big day.

The next day she called Vikram. Her name flashing on his mobile screen made the love-struck boy hear violins in the background. Vikram felt silly, but perhaps love did strange things to people. A quick plan for a rendezvous was made.

He reported at the coffee shop a little early and found Juhi walking in from the opposite direction.

They both laughed as they recognised eagerness in each other's eyes and chatted happily over coffee. Draping her voice in the silkiest tone, Juhi asked Vikram if he enjoyed trekking in remote jungles. His eyes widened in amazement as he admitted to being a keen trekker. He was gushing about how nice it was to find her sharing the same interests when Juhi declared that she hated such outings, but would take it up just for his sake!

She then asked if he liked watching the Grand Prix on ESPN.

'Yes! Oh yes! I love it...' he replied enthusiastically.

Well... It was not her cup of tea but since Vikram liked it, she would try and understand the nuances of the sport, just for his sake!

As the evening progressed, the conversation shifted to food.

'Kebabs and fish fry are my favourite dishes,' Vikram shared. Juhi was a vegetarian by choice but promised to learn to cook all that, just for his sake!

Vikram's happiness knew no bounds. He was one lucky bloke to have met this dream girl who looked like a little goddess and had a big heart. Vikram wanted to know if there was anything he could do for her.

Viola! This was her precious chance and she grabbed it with both hands. She whispered shyly if he could just do away with his moustache... It would make her extremely happy. As the gravity of her request dawned on him, Vikram realised that he was already knee-deep in quicksand.

Vikram was in low spirits for the rest of the evening. The warm, cosy feeling on his upper lip would be a thing of the past. The thought of how bare he would feel was depressing.

The wedding day arrived. Vikram sat on a white mare and looked majestic in his princely clothes. A headgear with little pearls strung together and a lovely sehra of white jasmine buds adorned his face. Once he was in close proximity to his beautiful bride, he lifted his sehra for her to catch a glimpse of his face.

Juhi remembers those dashing looks that floored her. But what she cherishes is that Vikram's love for her surpassed his love for his moustache. It was indeed a big sacrifice… Just for her sake!

Priyanka Kadam

Pickled

Nivedha's marriage was arranged with Kumar, a brilliant software engineer settled in San Francisco. During the brief courtship period of one month, they had spoken over the telephone a couple of times but Kumar had always been inhibited and shy. She wondered if he realised that his aloofness made him more attractive.

With the blare of loud Nadaswaram music in the background, Nivedha and Kumar tied the knot in a simple wedding ceremony. Nivedha glowed with the freshness of a bride. She sneaked occasional glances at her handsome groom who would smile and look away.

For the next two days, the house was bustling with relatives. Kumar felt self-conscious and his face coloured every time his wife looked at him flirtatiously.

They were getting ready to leave for the US and Kumar watched helplessly as his new bride cramped the bags with clothes, curios, condiments and other unnecessary items. It was only when he noticed a big jar of pickle that he gently expressed his disapproval.

'What? Paati made it with so much affection! You don't expect me to leave it?'

Kumar hesitantly explained how the extra baggage would be thrown out and that pickles could be messy and moreover, the immigration people might even object.

'Well, then that goes for the murukkus too,' she retorted, pointing to a large packet of coiled lentil biscuits which was Kumar's favourite snack. 'I insist on taking the pickle. I cannot break my Paati's heart,' she continued adamantly.

Kumar frowned and walked away and Nivedha was upset at the argument.

On the day of their departure, amidst weighing and tying of bags, Nivedha found it hard to control her tears.

'Have you wrapped the pickle properly and concealed it in the suitcase?' Kumar asked her. Nivedha nodded her head, relieved to hear him speak to her.

That evening, after a lot of tears and hugs, they left for the airport. They felt nervous as they stood in the line for the immigration procedure and baggage declaration. They would have to lie about the pickle.

The formalities were fulfilled smoothly. Nivedha gave a winning smile and Kumar heaved a huge sigh of relief as they boarded the aircraft. It was a long flight and both of them slept through it.

It was a tiring journey, but once they reached their charming little apartment in San Francisco, Nivedha felt her excitement building up. The next day, with renewed energy, she began the colossal task of unpacking. The moment she opened her suitcase, there was a drift of a pungent odour.

'Can you smell something?' she sniffed and asked Kumar.

'Yes, I can smell pickle!' Kumar replied with wide accusing eyes. He dug into the suitcase and pulled out Nivedha's favourite white kurta which now had big bright yellowish-orange oil patches on it. The oil from the pickle had leaked. He looked at Nivedha with an expression that said 'I told you so!' Nivedha stared at her kurta with dismay and held back her tears. She was the one who had insisted on bringing the pickle.

As Kumar carefully lifted the jar of pickle, Nivedha pulled out the packet of murukkus triumphantly. It was crushed to powder. They looked at each other mockingly and then Nivedha broke into a hearty laugh. Kumar couldn't help but smile at the sight of his beautiful wife laughing like a child. With an impish grin he pulled Nivedha towards him, enclosing her in his strong arms. This time it was the bride who blushed and looked away.

Pushpa Ramchandran

The Reincarnation of Mrs Bennet!

Overnight, there was a change in my mother. She had turned into Mrs Bennet! It had been difficult to struggle alone on life's thorny path for years now with her three daughters. Her eldest daughter had turned twenty-one, and was still unmarried! Maybe that is what triggered the change and set alarm bells ringing. The subtle whispers of well-meaning relatives forced her to dig deep into matrimonial columns, umpteen 'horror'scopes, and endless conversations with mothers who claimed to be authorities on the subject!

'Dee, there is this naval guy who is doing very well for himself, and his ship is now in port. He wants to settle down!' I sneaked information to my sister.

'Well, why doesn't he... Preferably at the bottom of the sea?' Dee replied rebelliously. She had no intention of being part of a harem, as the gory tales went, about sailors having a wife in every port!

But Mom looked so hopeful with her pleading kohl-filled eyes that Dee relented to an unusual viewing-the-girl setting. Mom and Dee set off on a moped to meet the boy and his parents. Dee was clad in a skirt. The boy and his parents gaped at the vision of the modern bride. 'She is too young, let her grow up a little!' came the verdict, as Dee sent up a prayer in relief, like a flare into the sky.

The next viewing was at home. No more skirts! The boy and his family were from America, well settled and well accented. Dee sat modestly in a neatly pinned heavy sari, the family jewellery in clear view, doing everything right (she had seen many too many Bollywood movies not to be perfect). Soon, the discussion moved onto to trickier ground and matrimony turned into matters of money. The boy and his family moved out as soon as Mom pronounced her daughter as the biggest dowry she could give. It was obviously not big enough to tempt Mr America! Another flare was sent up to heaven by a thankful Dee!

The next one was a pompous prospective groom with his ultra-conservative parents who saw no reason for one little woman to defy them. 'Our son is a brilliant catch!' the father remarked as the image of a fish flashed across all our minds. 'We do not want the girl to work after marriage as we have enough money to keep her happily at home!' he continued self-importantly.

The girl objected, 'How do you know I'll be happy with your son?' It was obviously the wrong question, at the right time! As the slighted boy and his family stomped out, a sheepish Mom refused to catch her daughter's quizzical eye. Another flare went up...

As the parade went on, the list wilted and so did poor Mom! With more and more flares going up, maybe God Himself started feeling the heat, and one fine day, a gallant young

Army officer walked into our home to pick up his aunt, a friend of Mom's, who had been visiting us. He charmed Mom completely with his dimples and impeccable manners, and impressed us with natural ease. As for Dee, she seemed to have decided not to send up any more sparkles!

Mom's list was finally thrown away, as she prepared to welcome her son-in-law into her heart and hearth! Mrs Bennett would go into hibernation ... for the next five years at least!

Deepti Menon

The Search

My father had three simple criteria for the bridegroom he was looking for me. The boy had to

- *Be a Ph.D.*
- *Be settled outside India (it didn't matter whether it was USA or Uzbekistan)*
- *Be Indian (he had started off with Bengali but my sister and I forced him to broaden the scope)*

I was not too sure about the basis of these criteria but he was adamant.

My father took the daunting task of looking for a suitable groom all upon himself. He started by placing an ad in the matrimonial columns of the local newspaper and spread the word around amongst the friendly neighbourhood aunts.

A distant aunt brought the proposal of a boy from the UK who was in India for a few days, and a meeting was arranged at our house. My part in the whole process was briefed to me. I would move towards the elders, touch their feet, smile at the others, take a seat near a corner and wait for further instructions.

The prospective groom arrived with his mother who looked harried. They had taken a rickety taxi and got stuck in a traffic jam that had given her a severe headache. After exchanging a few pleasantries, she actually asked if she could lie down in a room! We were gracious hosts and were glad to let her. I hung around in the kitchen.

Our maid, who had been sent to the shop, came with the sweets and samosas and on seeing the lady in my room asked me in whispers who she was. I responded cheekily that it was the groom's mother. The maid rolled out her eyes and gasped. Times were bad and turning worse, but a prospective groom's mother coming and lying down in the room...?

When I was called to the living room, I saw two gentlemen sitting there. One of them was probably the groom's father and I promptly moved over to touch his feet. As soon as I bent down, the gentleman flushed and almost shrieked! My father tersely told me that he was the prospective groom and I might want to touch his father's feet, though. I glanced at him and realized that he wasn't that old after all. God had not been kind with the hair follicles on his head but the face definitely was that of a young man. How stupid and careless of me!

I took my seat. The sweets and snacks arrived and the boy attacked a big samosa with an ambitious gulp when my father asked him 'Tumi kotota bangla bojho (How well do you understand Bengali)?' Apparently the conversation was happening in English till that point and father thought it was time to switch to our mother tongue.

In an attempt to respond quickly, while swallowing the samosa, he squealed! We realised after a few seconds that he was choking. Immediately, his father starting pounding him on the back and my father started fanning him while the maid brought some water. It was some time before he regained his composure. The whole house was in a tizzy except the probable groom's mother who groaned and went back to sleep. After fifteen minutes, she woke up and the party left.

The next day my father conveyed to them that we were not interested for various reasons.

Our maid was very happy about the decision though. 'What kind of a mother is this,' she wondered aloud, 'who comes to see a prospective bride and goes to sleep in their bedroom and does not even bother when the son is choking? And you know, she was watching me with half-closed eyes!'

My father was upset and blamed me for the mayhem that started when I touched his feet, unexpectedly. Soon everything was forgotten and father went back to looking for more prospects, and I looked forward eagerly to similar episodes.

Sutirtha Saha

7

FUNNY TALES

To keep your marriage brimming with love in the wedding cup, whenever you're wrong, admit it; whenever you're right, shut up.

—Ogden Nash

A Wife in Every Port

When Preeti married Shishir, everyone warned her against it. After all, he was a sailor. And it was no secret that a sailor has a wife in every port! But relationships are based on trust and as she had known him since she was little, she ignored the gossips of her home town folks and tied the knot.

As luck would have it, Shishir's ship was to sail to Europe and the couple were to honeymoon there. For someone who had never stepped out of the country, and more importantly sailed on a ship, Preeti couldn't have been happier. She took to life at sea and the days passed with ease.

However, the shock came when they called at their first port in Hamburg. While husband and wife strolled on the dock, a young boy with brownish hair and similar eyes, pretty much like Shishir's, came running towards them screaming, 'Papa, papa!' The moment he reached Shishir, he wrapped his arms around his legs and wept bitterly, speaking in a foreign tongue but repeating the word 'papa' continuously.

Preeti arched her eyebrows and looked at her few-weeks-old

husband. Papa? The similarity between the two hadn't gone unnoticed either.

Desperate to explain and reassure her, Shishir frantically tried to pry the child away, constantly calling out 'I am not your papa, go away' and turning to his scowling wife and saying 'Believe me, I don't know him'.

But the child was adamant. He brushed his tear-smeared face against Shishir and refused to let go. And just as Preeti was wondering whether or not she had been wise to ignore the old gossips of her home town, a woman, obviously this boy's mother, came puffing along, waving her arms.

'I'm sorry, I'm sorry,' she apologised as she dragged her weeping son away. 'He's mistaken you for his father whom he hasn't seen for a while,' she explained in broken English, cajoling the still sobbing child.

That explanation was more than enough for Shishir to plead his innocence and he said, 'That's ok, but take him away.' And he then pointed to Preeti and said 'wife'. The lady understood, apologised to Preeti and took her son away.

Preeti watched as Shishir finally heaved a sigh of relief. She smiled because she knew from that moment on that life with him would always be full of surprises! And it has been so!

Richa Wahi

'Chor' on My Plate

I married a guy who comes from a matriarchal family. And in that 'Nair' family structure, the maternal uncle is probably the most important person in your life after your parents. So after my marriage, I went to Kerala to meet my husband's only surviving maternal uncle and his family. That was my first visit to God's own country. In addition to the excitement of discovering a new place, there was also a sense of apprehension, a kind of uneasy feeling about whether I would fit in there (I am from East India who had lived in Delhi for quite some years before tying the knot).

My husband is the one who loves to play pranks and I have always been the victim of his pranks (which he calls innocent mazak). No matter how much I convince myself that I won't believe him, I end up doing that. The moment we got down from the auto (because his ancestral house didn't have a motorable road right up to the door), my husband kept on showing one house or the other telling me that that's his house. But I walked quite a bit (of course this was not a Dandi March) before I managed to enter into the house. There was a warm welcome sans any hugs (unlike Punjabis, Keralites are restrained in showing physical affection in any form).

Coming from Orissa, I was definitely used to seeing natural beauty, endless green fields and hundreds and hundreds of coconut trees standing elegantly. But even at first glance, Kerala looked quite intoxicating and sparklingly clean. The houses fitted beautifully with the lush green landscape (my husband's village is yet to be a victim of Dubai-enabled concrete obsession in Kerala).

After a nice bath, I was treated to soft idlis with sambar and coconut chutney and after years I actually loved the welcome break from toasted bread with jam or aloo/gobhi parathas at breakfast. Though I am not at all an idli fan, I still relished them. Though I was a daughter-in-law, nobody expected me to do any household work (which was a real blessing, I must admit). So, I happily sat down in the verandah with a glass of filter coffee and read the newspaper.

And then, around noon, as I was relaxing in my mother-in-law's room on the first floor (she doesn't live there but she's quite possessive about her ancestral space), suddenly my husband's uncle told me from the ground floor, 'Deepika, chor endaka.' Immediately, I jumped out of my bed thinking, 'Oh my God! What an exciting place! They even have thieves coming here in the middle of the day.' Living alone in Delhi had made me extra alert. So even without batting an eye-lid, I picked up a wooden stick lying around the room with the thought that I might get a national bravery award for my commendable act right here in my sasural.

When my husband saw me with the stick, he just couldn't understand why I was looking so charged up. I enthusiastically told him, 'I want to teach the thief a good lesson which he will remember throughout his life.' Seeing a quizzical look on his face, I told him, 'Oh, Mama just called out "chor"'. My husband just could not control his laughter and then he looked at me and said, 'Madam Jhansi ki Rani, please keep away that stick. Mama asked whether you will have rice or not for lunch. Chor in Malayalam means rice.'

This 'brave' act of mine became the talking point at lunch and everybody had a hearty laugh. And in many ways, this also broke the barrier between our two distinct worlds. When language is a barrier in expressing emotions, laughter comes as a great help. It did that to me in the new home which I had chosen for myself. After living in Delhi for years, subconsciously I had picked up food habits, sensibilities and much more of north India. But then in my one week's stay in Kerala during the month of December, I did not really miss my all time favourite aloo gobi and gajar ka halwa. I was happy eating eriserry, sambar, puttu and asking for more.

And needless to say, I had my entire life's quota of tender coconut water in that one week.

Deepika

Confusion

I was getting married after being engaged for six months. Being posted in Bosnia, I did not get the chance to meet my fiancé after the engagement ceremony. The modes of communication in those days were limited, so we hardly spoke, but I did know that she was as excited as I was about our coming together. As I sat in the mandap waiting for her, I dreamt of a wonderful honeymoon with my bride.

She looked stunning as she was escorted to the mandap by her sisters and friends, who of course blocked any chance of an eye contact with her. She came and sat next to me without acknowledging my presence. I was a little fazed but consoled myself by believing that she had probably been briefed to be shy on her wedding day. I kept sneaking glimpses of her through the corner of my eye, ruining all my wedding photographs where it appeared that I had a squint!

Suddenly, I noticed that she had been sniffing for a while. I turned my head to see that her eyes were swollen and watery and her nose was red. I got worried. 'In the last few days, had she had a change of heart?' My mind was racing with all kinds of thoughts. I was concerned and extremely upset. Her timidity and the hundreds of eyes watching us discouraged me from asking her what the matter was. My anxiety grew and I had no choice but to wait.

I longed for the crowd to diminish so that I could snatch a private moment with my bride, but it didn't happen. As directed by the pandit, I took her hand in mine and repeated the mantras. I vowed to take care of her for the rest of our lives, but couldn't muster the courage to ask her the reason she had been crying.

We were married. It was not until the wee hours of morning that we were finally alone in my room. As soon as I closed the door, I bombarded her with questions. 'Why have you been crying? Are you not happy with this marriage? Have you had a change of feelings while I was gone for six months? Do you want ...' I went on.

'Hold on... I am fine. What are you talking about?' She looked flustered.

'I am worried sick about how upset you have been. Please tell me what the matter is. Your eyes are swollen and wet with tears. Your face is red,' I explained nervously.

'Oh!' she exclaimed, blowing her nose loudly, 'that is because I have a terrible cold!' she replied matter-of-factly.

I grinned sheepishly as she looked at me with enquiring eyes. I told her about all the possible disasters I had thought of, in the last few hours, and we had a hearty laugh. I was overjoyed to have at last united with my bride with the rosy nose and swollen eyes, forever!

Veerendra Mishra

I Surrender

I didn't exactly realise what I was getting into when I had said 'yes' to Arjun under a sky of glittering diamonds. I was sitting on his lap on the terrace, wearing his favourite shorts. My hair was totally dishevelled. The green streaks were giving way to a pathetic dirty yellow but it was too dark to see. We were quite drunk when he popped up a totally unexpected question! Yes, yes, yes! And in that state of drunken stupor, I sent a spontaneous message to almost everyone on my contact list, saying that I am getting married to Arjun. Unfortunately, what I hadn't quite realised at that time was that 'almost everyone' would include all my cousins, my aunts and uncles and most importantly my mom and dad — a mistake I realised the next morning.

It was around one in the afternoon when I finally woke up to Esha's call when she asked me, 'Are you serious?'

'About what?'

'Marriage and Arjun…What else?'

My relationship with Arjun had eventually taken quite a serious turn and we both knew that our 'happily ever after' would be with each other. But why should that matter so suddenly to her was something I couldn't quite figure out while battling the hangover.

'Yaaaa, why?'

'So how did he ask you?'

In the meanwhile, I saw I was getting another call from an aunt (who doesn't usually call, mind you), so I put Esha on hold.

'Hello?' I said, quite inquisitive to know the reason for her sudden interest in me.

'Are you serious?'

No 'hello', no 'hi', no greeting whatsoever except a question that quite echoed Esha's opening statement. I was stunned.

She repeated her question.

'Are you serious?'

And I asked suspiciously, 'About what?'

'Marriage… Arjun… What else?' she replied in quite a matter of fact manner.

'How did you know?' I asked. As far as I knew, all she had been aware of was that Arjun was a friend, not even someone I was dating.

'Your message, you silly! I saw it in the morning!'

It was that one moment when everything that happened last night came back to me. I simply disconnected the line.

It was then that I saw how many people had tried contacting me since morning: I had sixteen missed calls and twenty-three messages. The last one was from Arjun, only half an hour back. I thought his could be the most comforting, and clicked the open message button. It said 'ur dad cald.m @ ur home nw.wake up n cme out asap.still luv u no matr wat'.

I wanted to die. At that exact moment my mother barged in. 'Your aunt's calling. Please come out after you finish, almost everyone's here. Some got your message, Dad called some,' she said with such a deadpan look on her face that I knew that there would definitely be a storm after that calm.

I creeped out of the room, trying not to imagine what might be the fate of my truly beloved, when I heard lots of loud voices coming from the drawing room. Panic struck. I felt as if I would definitely get a heart attack. I waited a second for me to fall. Nothing happened. I knew I had to go on, move on and face them all. The voices were laughter. I knew that it was an indicator that this whole marriage thing had been accepted, that I wouldn't be eaten alive. Yet my steps were calculated and slow. Though I was totally dry, I felt wet, being drenched in a sudden shower of total embarrassment. Always the tomboy daredevil, I had never been like this, but little was I to know how everything was to change, how differently I would be perceived from now on, how nameless I would become, how I would be just another bride.

'Arrey, still in shorts? Go and wear a salwar at least!'

'I didn't realise how fast she had grown up! Beautiful!'

'I have found this nice new sari shop, we'll buy the wedding sari there.'

'You have to notify the mehendiwali, it's the marriage season.'

'Wedding cards!'

'What about the venue and the menu?'

'Marriage registrar has to be informed.'

'First thing, black hair! Then beauty parlour... Oh my God, the beautician has to be booked!'

It took me a while to grasp everything that was happening. In the midst of a rather bad headache, I saw my marriage going out of my hands. All my relatives seemed like faces without names, personifying excitement. A play was to unfurl and they all had their parts. I would be given my lines soon. All I had to do was memorise and deliver. I had signed up for the part of the heroine, without knowing what I was in for.

Last night, we had planned our marriage.

'We'll get married in a yellow submarine.'

'In denim shorts.'

'We'll have a seven-tiered cake.'

'And chicken patties from Flury's.'

'I want heart-shaped balloons in pink.'

'Wouldn't that be too childish?'

'I guess…'

'Let's have a champagne tower.'

'Yup! And we'll exchange silver peace rings.'

'Let's promise each other our eternal love, right now.'

I thought that was a brilliant idea and we made rings out of cigarette foils. We got engaged and we kissed.

'You're a dreamer.'

'But I'm not the only one.'

Initially all their eyes were on me, but as soon as they started bombarding me with statements and questions, they got lost in their own words in their own thoughts. I stole that moment and glanced at Arjun. He kept looking at the floor with a permanent grin on his face. Though we had won a certain war without fighting, he knew I would have to wage a lot many more wars to get it all perfect, a word which was becoming more and more difficult to define. And he knew I would eventually have to surrender.

The closer we came to the wedding day, the lesser I got to meet Arjun and the more irritated I became. I wasn't a niece or cousin or grand-daughter anymore, I had become the bride who always had to smile. I realised that the family I called my own would officially not be mine anymore. I had to smile. People flocked to my home and invaded my privacy. I had to smile. My yellow submarine, shorts, cakes, patties, champagne fountain, silver peace rings, everything my dreams were made of, were shattered and replaced with banquets, Benarasis, diamonds, kebabs, mithais, mehendi… I had to smile. But strangely, my smile had begun hurting me. My cheeks ached. My heart ached. I was anything but a blushing bride. But each time I thought of Arjun, I felt happy and every day passed by as I kept sipping an extra large serving of a new and strange drink — an emotional cocktail.

'So much so for our yellow submarine,' I whispered to Arjun as we bid goodbye to our last guests at the wedding reception. I looked into his eyes and said apologetically, 'Your dreamer surrendered!' He smiled and said, 'Yes, to love.'

Joie Bose

Man in Blue

In Indian weddings, I wonder why everyone dresses up in such a way that each one looks like a bride or a bridegroom. This does not make it any easier for an absent-minded person like me who is terrible at remembering faces.

When I was in school, I would lend things to one girl and ask the other to return it. I didn't learn my lesson then, as lessons are always learnt the hard way, and with me it was the embarrassing way.

Being an arranged marriage, I met my fiancé just once before the wedding. We lived in different cities and immediately after our engagement, he had to travel abroad on an assignment. We did speak frequently over the phone but he came back two months later, just a day before the wedding.

It was the big day and I was escorted to the mandap by my brother. I looked up a few times to get a glimpse of my man, but his face was covered by a sehra. I noticed the colour of his sherwani, which was a beautiful hue of turquoise blue, an unusual colour for the groom.

After the ceremony, I was taken inside to freshen up and then, accompanied by my sister-in-law, to the lunch table. I spotted my 'man in blue' and went and sat beside him. He smiled uncomfortably at me. Everybody was staring at me. But they had been doing it since the beginning of the day so I was unperturbed. My sister, sitting opposite me, signalled with her eyes. I couldn't understand what she wanted to tell me, so I smiled and ignored her.

My sister then stood up and announced loudly, 'We are going to play a game before lunch for which we need to have the bride and groom sitting together, so Anu can you please come and sit here next to Rishi?' She was pointing to an empty chair next to another 'man in blue'. I was stunned and looked carefully at the guy sitting next to me. Oh God! His was definitely not the face I had seen in the photograph of Rishi that I possessed!

Without a word I got up and walked towards Rishi. I wanted to kick myself for being so lost and inattentive every time, especially today!

After a few days, I confessed my folly to Rishi who had a hearty laugh and now, a reason to tease me every now and then. But the one good thing that came out of this incident is that now when I see a face, I never forget it, ever!

Aparana Shankar

Meeting the In-Laws

There were no blessings from India. We had a registered wedding, and our reception was coffee and cake in a nearby snack-bar. This rather bleak start to our marriage was not as inauspicious as it might seem. We were determined to make a success of it. But we had work to do: I returned to college to complete a course in textile design while Arun finished his Institute of Mechanical Engineers exams. We met at weekends… And two months later, I found out I was pregnant!

Having weathered his parents' wrath, Arun gave in to their pleas to return to India, and started job-hunting. I was happy to follow him there, only asking that he stay till the baby was born. I went home after my final exams, and had him to myself for a month. Arun saw his daughter just an hour after she was born; she looked up at him with that mysterious, hazy gaze that newborns have, curled her tiny hand round his finger, and fell asleep. He was literally hooked!

Arun left for India at the end of October. I came by sea when Madhu was four months old, a fifteen-day voyage (a holiday! but oh, so lonely!) via the Suez Canal, so that we could get acclimatised. The night before we arrived, I was unable to sleep for excitement. My first sight of India was the Gateway of India, shining above the winter morning mist. The ship docked at Ballard Pier, which was impossibly crowded. I wondered how I would ever find Arun in this noisy melee, and it was then that I realised what an enormous step I had taken. Miraculously, he was there beside me! I was so overcome with relief, I fell into his arms and burst into tears.

Surprisingly, my bottle of Champagne was listed as cologne by the customs officer. There was no duty! Then we took a taxi to Arun's masi's flat on Marine Drive. Shrouded bodies lay in deep slumber on the pavements. Naively, I assumed they were waiting for a boat...

I stood shyly in the drawing-room, holding Madhu. The maid-servants patted her cheeks, asking, 'Baby ya Baba?'

'Boy or girl?' translated Arun,

'Oh... Baby,' I said. I had just had my first Hindi lesson.

Masi served us breakfast of halva with puris, a celebration breakfast, said Arun. They were celebrating me! It was a wonderful feeling.

What a wonderful, relaxed period. Cocooned by a loving family, I learned simple Hindi, how to manage servants, and basic Punjabi khana. Masi gave me my first sari. I found my way around Mumbai. I wrote letters every week to my parents and to my in-laws. I had no time to be homesick!

Then Arun's cousin invited us to his wedding in Delhi: I was to meet my in-laws for the first time. Arun couldn't go... Nervously, I went by train, with Madhu, now eleven months old. Arun's Mami spent two days teaching me to be a model bahu before my in-laws arrived. That fateful morning, I was sent to the hairdresser, and my waist-long hair was piled into a mountain held in place by hundreds of pins, which slithered out at every opportunity. I wore one of my two saris, and stood ready to greet my in-laws as instructed.

'They've come!' called out Mami, watching from the window. I positioned myself, and realised there was not enough pallu to cover my head. The doorbell rang, and at that point Madhu pulled herself up, clutching the pleats of my sari and pulling them out. I was in a complete panic. My in-laws opened the door for themselves, to find me clutching my pleats with one hand and fending off Madhu with the other. I waved my hand quickly at them and said, 'Hi!' in a flustered voice. I could not say 'Namaste', I could not cover my head, and neither could I bend to touch their feet, in case my hairdo fell off. Mami was in fits of helpless laughter.

I enjoyed an occasional cigarette, and as we sat and chatted after lunch, I politely offered one to my father-in-law. There was instant, frozen silence. My father-in-law said, slowly and stiffly, 'We - don't - smoke.' I hastily put the cigarettes away, but I could see them glancing meaningfully at each other. Mami quickly decided it was time for me to feed Madhu and hauled me off to her room.

'Arun told me his father smoked!' I said indignantly.

'Well, he did, once,' said Mami, 'but young people don't smoke in front of their elders.' She began to laugh. 'Did you see their faces?' she said.

Was I ever going to forget them? But I could see the funny side of it. We lay on the bed and laughed ourselves silly at my faux pas.

That afternoon my in-laws took me shopping for saris. After

some nudging from Mami, they also bought me some jewellery. A tailor came to make blouses and petticoats. Delicately, he measured me, marked and cut out the cloth, and took the pieces away for stitching, to be ready the next day.

In the evening, a dust-storm threatened. We sat in Mami's room with everything tightly shut; even so, the air slowly turned a reddish brown. Suddenly rain roared down. The doors and windows were opened, and there was the smell of freshly wetted earth. It continued to rain for about an hour. It became dark.

'Who wants a drink?' called out Mami.

'I do!' I said. I definitely needed that drink!

She hesitated. My in-laws wore expressions that said, so she drinks as well! But I had decided that by now nothing could get worse. So I had my drink, and Mami had a drink, and the cousin-to-be-married had a drink, and in the end so did my father-in-law. Then we had dinner, and went to bed.

That night, as we lay in the wide bed with Madhu between us, Mami said, 'Well, now they know the worst. And you know what not to do.' Then she lectured me on what I should do: The next day all the Delhi relatives were coming for tea.

At the tea-party, Mami's maid carried Madhu around to be introduced to some fifty relatives. Arun's first child, said Mami, beaming, daring them to commiserate with my in-laws that she was a girl. I handed out cups of tea and various delicacies. My sari did not fall off, and my hair was sprayed rigid. I did not offer anyone a cigarette! The wedding too was a success; I had begun to learn names and relationships. My in-laws thawed. By the time they left for Jammu, we had established a cautiously friendly relationship.

I returned to Mumbai to find that news of my dreadful first day had already reached Arun and Masi, who burst into laughter every time it was mentioned.

'O my!' said Arun's cousin. 'You actually offered Uncle-ji a cigarette? And had a drink?'

'Worse!' I said cheerfully, and told her about the un-tucked sari and the collapsing hair. She was impressed that I had survived the disaster.

For Madhu's first Diwali, we went to stay with Arun's parents in Jammu. Arun returned to work, but Madhu and I stayed back, as my in-laws wanted us to meet all their friends. In December, I returned home by train, and at New Delhi station learned of the earthquake in Mumbai.

Aw shucks, I said to myself. I missed my very first earthquake!

But Mumbai was still trembling when Arun collected me off the train, and continued to do so for several days. Arun reckoned, though, that nothing could have been as earth-shaking as that first meeting with my in-laws!

Jane Bhandari

Queen for the Day

Though I am talking of a wedding, the above honour does not refer to the bride or the all-powerful mother of the groom. It is about one of the guests brimming with self importance and looking down contemptuously on us — the bride's people.

The groom's mother made a not-so-unusual demand, that two of the guests, in fact, her sister and her daughter-in-law, were coming by the state transport bus and reaching around 11 p.m.; could someone from the girl's side go to the bus station and bring them to the wedding hall?

Well, being the girl's people and the hosts, ours was not to question as to why two women should travel to reach at an unearthly hour and why they could not have taken a day bus. We meekly said 'Yes'.

As the guests were females and since they might have reservations about being received by strange men, I agreed to accompany my nephew and the driver to the bus stop.

We reached about half-an-hour before time and waited. The bus arrived half-an-hour late. All the passengers alighted and the duo was missing!

We did not know what to make of it. Had they got down at some earlier stop and were stranded now at a deserted bus stop, inviting all kinds of unsavoury elements? And ladies generally load themselves with gold when they attend a wedding.

My nephew made a frantic phone call to the boy's mother about her missing sister and demanded her mobile number. After sleepily rummaging through her hand bag and other effects, she dished out the number asking us to keep her informed about the development. My nephew could not make out anything of her weary cry of 'Oh, trust that woman to create a mess' and a male voice (we learnt afterwards that it was the father of the groom) interpolating 'and do not bring them to our quarters when you do find them'. But later on, the meaning became only all too clear.

After some five unsuccessful attempts with our hearts in our mouths, the mobile responded. When we asked where they were, the lady replied casually, 'On the bus, where else? We will be reaching in another hour or so. We missed the earlier bus and since you people will anyway be at the bus stop for sure, we did not worry. Stay there to receive us.'

My nephew was frothing at the mouth and was raring to retort.

I had to remind him that he was the bride's brother and it would not be in good taste to start an argument.

It was two in the morning when we reached the wedding hall with the truant guests.

The lady informed us that she was in no shape to climb the stairs to the first floor and told us to requisition the lift. (She was a woman just in her late forties and obviously in perfect form!)

The passenger lift was closed for the night and we hunted out the person who manned the service lift. My nephew looked at me gleefully when he accommodated her among bundles and bundles of plantain leaves meant for the kitchen.

She said, 'Give us coffee and a few biscuits at least. I am sure breakfast is hours away.'

Fortunately, a niece of mine had a flask of hot water and a bottle of Horlicks for her baby. I made the drink and my nephew produced a few bananas from nowhere.

'Now for sleeping arrangements,' she said and with a cursory glance to the room allotted for the bride's side, moved briskly to the only cot available, prodded the sleeping man in the ribs, ordered him to get off and royally occupied it asking her daughter-in-law to make herself as comfortable as she could and went off to rhythmic snoring.

(A few of us close relatives had decided to stay back in the wedding hall for the night, squeezing ourselves into a single room whereas the rest of the guests were booked in hotels.)

My husband who was the dislodged sleeper blinked for a few moments and went to lie down in the middle of a mound of suitcases. Later on, he said that it was a good thing that his wife had trained him well to obey orders unquestioningly and not waste time in futile arguments!

At six in the morning, after having been served coffee, she evacuated all men as well as women from our room, took her own time bathing and dressing up, and ordered her daughter-in-law too to get ready. When she came out at last, she told us curtly not to keep the room closed for long as she could not stand out for a protracted period of time. My nephew pointedly brought two chairs and waved them to be seated.

The daughter-in-law whispered to me, 'Don't pay any attention to her, that only makes her more tyrannical.'

I learnt from her how, for Preethi did not show any sign that she heard any of her mother-in- law's instructions or queries and pretended to lend her ears to the nadhaswaram. (instrumental music played on south Indian weddings). I loved the girl. She was a survivor!

The woman explained to all and sundry that she and her daughter-in-law enjoyed an exalted status as the wedding guests. The reason was that the groom's side had a paucity of girls and Preethi was to be treated as the sister of the groom (by a long stretch of imagination) to officiate as the one to tie the third knot of the mangalsutra, a prerogative of the boy's sister.

By eight in the morning, the groom's side and other guests arrived at the wedding hall. The sisters acknowledged each other with a profuse show of affection and the brother-in-law nodded with a scowl. No love lost there. I was not surprised.

The groom's mother made an aside to me, 'Thank you for keeping her with you for the night. She is an overbearing woman. (Didn't we know!) My husband and she never stop quarrelling almost from the moment they come together.'

I could sympathise with the man.

The rest of the wedding went of fairly peacefully for us as even she had to acknowledge that her sister and her husband had more right to recognition and show of respect from us than she did and with so many guests around, the attention could not be monopolised any longer. Her daughter-in-law now became the sole target of her comments and commands, and needless to say that the latter paid scant attention.

The day after the wedding, when they were leaving, my nephew told the lady that there was no berth reservation available on the train back and she would have to sit up during the whole journey. I thought that it was mean of him to smile when he said that, but then he had every reason to have his back.

Revathi Seshadri

The Bridal Blouse

I was all of eighteen, very plump and desperately trying to lose weight, especially from my face.

So many times people would ask me what sweet are you sucking and I would say, no, these are just my cheeks which are so fat.

And then as they say, mera rishta pucca ho gaya. A family came to see me, they liked me for their son and wanted the marriage to take place soon.

My mom and dad were ecstatic, I was indifferent. I was busy reading Agatha Christie lying in bed and eating. Sometimes it would be such an effort to get up to put a wrapper or peel in the dustbin, I would just put it under the mattress.

The D-Day was fast approaching. There was a flurry of activity in the house, shopping was in full swing.

Needless to add, I was staying in a really small town, more like a village, where ideas, resources, exposure and everything else was limited. And this happened nearly thirty years ago.

My mom, my elder cousin and I went out shopping for me. My mom was very anti make-up. She thought beauty comes from within but still, my cousin, whom we thought was really fashionable, managed to persuade my mother to buy really pale, translucent, shimmery powder, pink lipstick, blue and green eye shadow, and everything else that would make me look as though I was the main lead in a Ramsay movie production.

My cousin's friend was going to apply mehendi on my hands.

The night before the wedding, she sat and made intricate and beautiful patterns on my hand and when she started working on my second hand, her baby started crying hysterically. It was a bad attack of colic. She left the second hand midway and ran to attend to her baby.

My cousin, through whom the same inartistic vein ran like mine, decided to complete the job. I am sure it was botchy but at that time, I thought the mehendi was wonderful.

My make-up was done by my bhabi and the same cousin.

I still remember them attaching a huge bouffant to my hair, which even to me seemed in urgent need of washing. I had got my wedding saree blouse stitched from Delhi, then the Mecca of all fashion. My cousin put the chalky white foundation that did not at all merge with my brown skin, and blue eye shadow, and then she put the eyeliner and took out the line way beyond my eyes like Mumtaaz or Waheeda Rehman, or whomever was her current favourite. In fact, she had pictures of these heroines in a wedding gear with her and she was trying to follow their make-up!

Finally, it was all done. I was ready to meet the bridegroom whom I had met just twice, once before the engagement and once during the engagement. After that, we had sent a couple of really childish letters and cards with sentimental mush written on them.

The baraat had come. The jaimala was done, the pheras were over and we were pronounced as husband and wife.

The first thing my husband said on looking at me, 'You look beautiful.' Forgotten was the smudged make-up which I am sure made me look like Dracula risen from the grave for the umpteenth time.

One blissful month of marriage passed. Though I was barely nineteen, I was crazily in love with my husband, my make-up abilities, household abilities were slowly becoming from zero to point one.

It is another matter that my husband was fairly appreciative of what I cooked and what I wore and gave me confidence.

Another of my cousins came down to meet me at this time.

Very excitedly, she wanted to go through my wedding album.

'Didi,' she screamed, 'you've worn your blouse the other way round! The buttons should have been behind.' And she showed how my blouse looked in the pictures, filled up at the back because that's where the katori protruded! I wondered what happened to my bhabhi and my cousin's make-up skills! Such a faux paus, and they missed it!

We collapsed in a paroxysm of laughter.

My husband came from the other room and asked why we were all laughing so much.

'Bhayia,' she laughed, 'you got very lucky.'

He raised a quizzical eyebrow. Thank god she did not spell it loudly — what a well endowed wife he had!

Anu Chopra

The Other Woman

Charu had never thought she would get married to an Air Force officer. She always thought them to be frivolous, unreliable and too flamboyant for her liking. With their Ray-Bans and snazzy overalls, she felt they were too 'forward' for her small town upbringing. Yet, in her deepest, innermost thoughts, she had never believed that it could happen to her.

Raman had seemed nice enough initially. However, from the moment they had returned to the squadron, he and his cronies seemed to be talking in whispers, conspiratorially. She could see something cooking, and did not like the flavour wafting from it. 'Surely they should have nothing to hide from me. After all, I am his wife,' she fumed.

It did not take long for the truth to surface. Within two hours, things started hotting up. Charu heard the sound of squealing tires and car doors being banged. This was followed by loud angry voices. Raman got up with a start and tried to flee. A huge guy barged into their drawing room, shouting for Raman, while his mates barred all exits. Raman had no choice but to stand rooted, looking uncomfortable and a trifle scared.

'You filthy bas***d,' the Big Guy abused her husband, as he protectively brought forth a meek little girl through the doorway. She was sobbing quietly, her large pregnant belly shaking with each sob. Her face was hidden in her duppatta and while Charu could not see it, she appeared completely shattered.

Big Guy was in a terrible rage. 'Did you ever think what would happen to my sister? How could you go and get married, after you have done this to her?' He moved forward menacingly, eyes bulging with anger, breathing fire. He thumped Raman hard on his chest and held him by his collar. Charu felt herself reeling and clutched a chair for support. She would have fallen, had a gentle hand not supported her.

She shifted her gaze to see an old lady looking at her benevolently. She spoke gently, 'Beta, we understand it is not your fault. I am sure that you knew nothing about this. But tell me, with my daughter in this state, what else can we do?' She pointed at the pregnant girl, with a meek question in her eyes. Charu, despite herself, felt a deep empathy for the girl.

'He has to marry her,' she heard the old lady saying vehemently.

Brought up in a household where infidelity and adultery were treated equivalent to rape, she could not believe this was happening to her. More than Raman, she felt angry with her father, who had disregarded her doubts and hitched her to Raman. It dawned very slowly on her that her life was utterly, completely ruined.

The desperation gave her strength. Turning a deaf ear to the other room where her husband of a few days was being roughed up, she stood before the old lady and her pregnant daughter.

'You are right. He must marry her. I will go to my father's house tomorrow. My hus...' her voice trailed off. 'Please ask Raman to send me the divorce papers to my father's place.'

The old lady looked satisfied with this. The commotion in the other room was increasing. Another set of voices had joined in. Charu peeped through the curtain to see Raman's cronies. Were they really trying to justify his despicable behaviour? Charu could have torn their eyes out; however, she remained quiet. The old lady quietly informed them of Charu's decision. She and Big Guy left with the pregnant girl.

'Let us go to the CO's house and talk this out,' Raman's cronies said lamely to Charu. She wanted to refuse but realised her own helplessness just in time. In an alien place, 500 km away from her father's house, without a friend, where would she go? She needed a place to stay the night. 'Oh God! Let the CO have some sense,' she prayed.

The CO turned out to be a venerable and reasonable man. He made her comfortable, offered her a glass of water and asked her to sit comfortably in his house. He assured her, then left in his jeep to talk to the pregnant girl's family.

He came back looking dejected. Back at his house, the CO tried to reason with Charu. 'Why don't you just wait a week and see? Maybe things would sort themselves out.'

Charu broke down. 'How can I spend a lifetime with such a scoundrel? He has done this to one girl today, he can do this to me tomorrow.' She was crying openly now, tears flowing down her cheeks. 'Please arrange for a ticket to my father's house,' she sobbed. The CO seemed perturbed by this. He called his wife to talk to her.

Things appeared to be happening in a blur now. Gradually, she seemed to have many more well wishers pouring in from all directions. Through her tears and numbed senses, some vague recognition started dawning.

All the people she had met since coming to Jwalapur were standing around her trying to shush her down. They seemed thick friends, despite the happenings of the day. Big Guy was introducing himself to her as the squadron doctor. The pregnant girl came and introduced herself as Mrs So-and-so along with her husband.

'Noooooo!!' she screamed, as the truth hit her. A similar thing had happened to her sister, when she got married to an Army officer. Charu had never believed that she would fall for such a clichéd ploy — but she had. She realised that Raman was involved as deeply in pulling the prank. She could have killed Raman then, except that the relief was so overwhelming. In the next few minutes she was introduced to the whole cast of the skit — all officers and wives from Raman's squadron — and of course, Raman's friend's mom, who had played the part of the girl's mother.

Today, Raman and Charu have been happily married for eighteen years. Since then, Charu too has played many a character trying to make each girl's honeymoon with the squadron more memorable.

Lona

Who is the Groom?

My aunt Meena was ready for marriage. Her parents had found a suitable groom for her but before that, the boy had to see the girl, and the girl's parents, relatives and neighbours wanted to see the boy. The girl's opinion did not really matter.

The entire village waited impatiently for the prospective groom, who finally arrived on a motor cycle with a friend. They were welcomed with much enthusiasm and served some buttermilk. An awkward silence followed until somebody suggested that the boy should see his future wife. 'He looks very eager and tense,' he remarked. Everyone laughed at the poor joke and the clearly embarrassed groom smiled politely.

Meena Aunty's face was being made up at feverish pace when her father came to take her outside. Sensing her uneasiness, he said, 'Meena, just because you are a girl, I don't want to force you into a marriage against your wishes. We will go ahead only if you like the boy.' It was a huge relief for her to know that her opinion did matter.

She walked out nervously into the crowded living room and after a few minutes, was asked to go back inside. The boy smiled and nodded his head as a sign of approval. The bride's father went inside and asked her, 'Meena, do you like him?' My aunt had managed to steal one glance at the boy and had liked what she saw. She nodded her head in agreement. Everybody was overjoyed and the wedding date was fixed for the next muhurtham (auspicious day).

The marriage ceremony had begun and Meena Aunty was escorted to the mandap by her sisters. They giggled and nudged her to take one look at the handsome bridegroom. She looked up shyly and was shocked. He was NOT the boy she had seen and agreed to marry, it was the boy sitting next to the groom. What was going on? She was flustered and confused but did not have the courage to speak up. They were married.

Well, the truth is that there was no mix-up of grooms. It is my aunt, who was so baffled at the time of the 'bride viewing' that she had mistaken the boy's friend as the groom-to-be!

It is only after a few years that Meena Aunty narrated this funny incident to her husband with a teasing comment that she should have married his friend.

'Impossible,' said my uncle as his wife looked at him curiously. 'I made sure I was accompanied by a friend who was already married!'

As the saying goes, all's well that ends well. Meena Aunty and her husband are happily married for forty years now, with wonderful children and plenty of grandchildren.

N. Chokkan

8

COOKED UP

The most wasted day is that in which we have not laughed.

–Chamfort

A Cooked-up Story

'What if they ask me to cook something?' was one of the first questions I asked my husband of a few hours. He laughed and said what he had been saying for the last two years that we were dating, 'Just say "no".' It was easier said than done, especially when you are in an atmosphere that's hostile, to put it mildly.

We were to spend the weekend with his family, before going to our own new place, for our new life. So I was on my best behaviour and hoped it didn't show. Suddenly I realised I was all alone in a home and family where I barely knew anyone. I am very different from them and clearly both sides were treading carefully. I must say they tried to make me feel welcome and I realised how the dynamics between the women in a family is what sets the tone. My husband was in the home he grew up in and obviously totally comfortable. The day passed off smoothly and my husband joked in private that I seemed to be enjoying the TV serial bahu role to the hilt! Must say it did feel good when at the dinner table my father-in-law made some stray comment on how once you get to know people, preconceived biases drop. My husband winked across the table. My mother-in-law asked someone to get almonds from the grocer as I was making halwa in the morning. I almost choked on the water I was drinking. She asked if everything was ok, I said I was good and of course I knew it was the custom.

This was tougher than preparing for any exam or presentation at work. My husband suggested we walk on the terrace. I tried to be brave but he could sense what was going on. We had our first argument as a married couple. He had no issues with the fact that I was a career oriented person who never had any interest or time to cook. I was missing my mom. She had spent the last ten years at least trying to get me to learn the basics of cooking and I always said I didn't have the time, I would marry a man who knew how to cook. Thankfully I had, so he spent the next two hours explaining how halwa was made. I revised, learnt it by rote and kept repeating the recipe over and over again. He never had, or never has, shown as much patience as he did that night.

We were both up and ready at the crack of dawn and he was wishing me luck and assuring me that I would do fine. I had to stop him from going and stopping his mom from calling off the plan. I was nervous and just hoping I wouldn't drop something or burn something and ruin my reputation for life. He promised to come and stand with me in the kitchen. I said no to that, just requested him to keep his brother's wife out.

My mother-in-law walked into the kitchen, with both of us following. She asked him to leave and said just she and her new daughter-in-law were permitted in today. Like all moms, she knew exactly what I was feeling. Yet once I started, she stood by me and short of making the halwa herself, did everything.

She kept giving me a running commentary on how it was done in their house and I just kept following her instructions to the T.

You know what happened next. The halwa was declared divine and all the elders in the family gave me money and gifts. On the way back home, my husband declared that he now knew that not just his mom but even his wife was a pretty good actress!

Shifa Maitra

Chef Supreme

I had cooked up a storm then in an old aluminium oven. It was one of the big, round, indigenously designed, ingenuous ones with a circular glass top and a plug-in point on one side, from which the wire hung its way to the power connection point on the wall. It was placed in the verandah outside the kitchen. I could enjoy the closeness of the kitchen and the availability of the ingredients and the fridge. I could also enjoy the late spring breeze, since it was March.

March is the month of my marriage. The wedding mehendi had not faded from my hands before my husband, in his totally happy just married state, threw a party for all his friends. Hearing that I was cooking (did I have a choice?), his younger sister invited all her friends as well. There was to be drinks and dinner.

The style of the late Seventies was bohemian, nothing predetermined, packaged or formal. We were young and carefree and our drinks and dinner parties were just like that: basic, wholesome and filled with fun and bonhomie.

It was a time when ethnic was in, so we wore lehengas and

anklets and kolhapuris and lolled against gautakiyas with kohl in our eyes. We nursed our dreams and had no pressures to provide for anyone. Yet, the pressure was on for me now, a subtle one, to serve up a good dinner.

Surprise! I had been spoilt rotten and did not know even the names of dals, only that some were yellow, others green and yet others black. And here I was, trying to cook, a whole leg of lamb. But I have authentic adventurous blood somewhere in my genes. So out came a thick recipe book with a glossy yellow cover, filled with recipes for dishes waiting to be cooked. I looked at the measures required and my eyes widened. The recipes had pounds and ounces written all over them. Luckily, the book did have conversion tables at the back, so I could work with tablespoons or gms. Totally relieved, I collected the ingredients.

The recipe required I use an oven. On hand and available was no MasterChef oven, but my sister-in-law had this nice fat round one I have been talking about, which she used for baking the occasional cake.

I thought now about what I was doing. I stared at the leg of lamb. It lay there, all pink and waiting to be spiced up.

I was being ambitious. I could have stuck to a more traditional dish like Rogan Josh and my mother- in-law would have helped. Newly married, I was kind of shy of her and also not very comfortable with the idea yet of cooking 'with' her. Also, I wanted this to be my dish, made solely by me, brimming over as I was with romance and love and a desire to prove my worth as a wife. Yes, that mattered then to me, a lot. I still believe that cooking is one way of expressing love, among the many ways we have.

So the meat was washed, and marinated in freshly ground spices, salt and yoghurt. Meanwhile, the oven was cleaned, oiled from the inside, and the leg of lamb gingerly placed within. It was to cook slow and steady and then turned on to the other side after a while. I opened the oven after some time and turned the leg gently over, basted it with some of the liquid sauce that had started forming around the leg, and then closed the lid again. The smells emanating from it were good, they were very good.

And then it was done. It was well browned from the top and the flesh was firm but juicy. The smell of spices filled the verandah and I closed the lid. I would remove it and decorate it later.

The dinner was a stupendous success. I was declared 'chef supreme'. I was a novice, but no one needed to know that. Cooking this dish was a completely new experience for me. However, I had followed the instructions carefully and put my heart and soul into the preparation. I blushed with all the compliments. The stars in my eyes were doubled by the proud and loving look in my husband's eyes.

Despite being 'just married', I had shown that I had it in me to tackle anything with gusto and confidence and deliver. I had also proved that a dish cooked with love tastes very good. A taste that is never forgotten even after years of marriage.

Abha Iyengar

First Attempt

As soon as I closed the door of my bedroom, tears streamed down my cheeks. I was going to make a complete fool of myself.

I dialled the helpline number on my phone. Before my mother could say anything, I started bawling. She comforted me and after a twenty-minute-long conversation in muted tones, I hung up feeling a little more confident.

I had been married for a month. My husband was a loud, fun-loving Punjabi while I was from a traditional south Indian family. Petty issues regarding language and food surfaced frequently but at the moment, I was faced with a serious dilemma.

There were guests coming home for dinner and I was expected to cook for them. It was not such a big deal, except that I had never cooked before! My mother had excellent culinary skills and the only way I benefitted from this was by having developed a great appetite. I was annoyed at myself for not having learnt how to cook, and for telling my mother-in-law that I could.

I got up and strode into the kitchen to find my mother-in-law preparing chapatis and my favourite palak paneer. She had been preparing delicious food for me every day.

'So have you decided what you would be cooking for dinner?' she enquired.

'Masala dosa, sambhar and coconut chutney,' I announced proudly as if these were names of exotic dishes unheard of to the common man.

At four o' clock, I started what seemed like a colossal task. My husband strolled in and out of the kitchen restlessly. He had a queer smile on his face to mask his nervousness.

Finally, after a huge effort at cooking, I began to wind up the clutter. I took three hours for an hour's work, but it was done. The guests arrived at 7.30 p.m. They spoke animatedly about how they had been looking forward to the dinner. We sat in the living room making trivial conversation and after twenty minutes, I excused myself and went to my bedroom. I switched on the television and stretched out my legs to loosen up before getting into a struggle with the dosa preparation.

'Hey, they are leaving. Come and say goodbye to them,' it was my husband calling out to me.

'Leaving, without eating?' I asked, rubbing my eyes.

He smiled and pointed his finger towards the clock. I was shocked. I had slept through the dinner.

'It is ten o'clock! Why didn't you wake me up?' I shouted at him.

'Honey, you looked tired after all that cooking so we decided not to disturb you,' he replied calmly with a smile.

I felt dreadfully ashamed of myself. How would I face them? What would they think about me?

'The food was awesome,' Maasi commented. 'We will come for dinner again next month,' she continued encouragingly. I smiled sheepishly.

After they left, I finished my dinner and was washing the plates, when my husband came in and remarked, 'The food was fabulous. I didn't know you could cook so well.' I looked at him for a minute.

'I can understand why Maasi said that; she obviously did not want to hurt me. But, you too? I have eaten the same food!' We burst out laughing.

Later in the night, I called my mother. She was worried and eager to know how the dinner was.

'Well ... the potatoes were not properly boiled, the chutney was too salty and the sambhar was thick and tasteless as I had used chana dal instead of toor dal.'

'And the dosa...?' she asked, trying to hold on to the little confidence she had in me.

'The dosas turned out well because they made it themselves as I fell asleep,' I replied slowly. My mom laughed.

I laughed at myself too and felt guilty, but deep inside I was overwhelmed by the support my husband and in-laws had shown. It was their way of letting me know that 'we are now a family'!

Vaishnavi Ankush Verma

Hosting My First Dinner Party

Thirty-one years of married life has brought with it a certain amount of familiarity and expertise in the kitchen. When half-a-dozen friends suddenly drop in for a bite or a horde of ravenous kids raid my larder, I take it in my stride. Over the years, I have learnt to concoct crunchy cutlets with leftover rice and veggies; whip up a strawberry milkshake for a reluctant little milk-drinker by simply adding a spoonful of jam to a glass of milk; bake cakes in a pressure cooker when the electricity fails; and turn around a disaster into an inspiration. It wasn't always like this...

As a new bride, I was an absolute novice in the art of cooking. Until my wedding, the kitchen was strange, uncharted territory for me. In ways I could never fathom, the tea in my hands turned to muddy brown water, the chapatis assumed the shapes of various countries on the world map, and when I tried my hand at a chocolate pudding, my brother, who often volunteered to be my guinea-pig, took one bite and hastily tipped the entire concoction into the garbage can 'before it poisoned the others'.

My mother predicted that if the adage 'the way to a man's heart is through his stomach' held true, my marriage would surely head for the rocks. But thankfully my husband believed that 'love is blind'. How else could he have survived my initial disasters?

With stars in his eyes and years of eating indifferently cooked Officers Mess food, he was ready to hand me the 'Best Chef Award' on a silver platter. He was delighted with my culinary skills and decided that he couldn't keep it solely to himself anymore. He would invite his Commanding Officer for dinner. Since this would be my first attempt at hosting my own dinner party, and I was not too sure of my capabilities, I explained that we should keep that for later.

'A little more experience would make the meal better,' I explained in words that actually meant, 'I don't want to poison your boss and damage your chances of a promotion.'

We decided to invite some other friends. A Sunday was fixed for the great event. Although it was a dinner, we set to work immediately after a hurried breakfast. The menu was not over-ambitious — chana, aloo dum, chicken curry, tomato chutney and custard pudding as dessert.

I began with the chana and referred to the instructions in the recipe book. The gram was boiled in the pressure cooker for twenty minutes, but still remained a trifle hard. I had forgotten to soak them overnight! Well, the tasty fried-onion masala would make up for that.

I then went on to boil the potatoes for the aloo dum. As the potatoes were larger than the chana, I presumed that they would take longer to cook. So I pressure cooked the carefully chosen round potatoes for forty minutes. What came out was potato pulp and shreds of its peels. My husband, four years older and wiser, advised me to keep the pulp aside. 'You never know, it might come in handy,' he said. And they did.

Off he went to buy another batch of potatoes while I worked on the two-legged bird. This was the main dish. I filled the cooker to the brim with water and added the tomatoes and spices. After the recommended twenty whistles (which I sat back and counted patiently), I opened the vessel only to find the chicken pieces swimming like some exotic fish in the watery gravy.

'Don't you worry,' said my helpful partner, squashing a grin, 'I'll dive in to retrieve the pieces.' That was all I needed to break into loud sniffles.

'Now, now,' he patted me comfortingly, 'just add those mashed potatoes and a little salt to thicken the gravy.' It worked.

With increasing nervousness, I battled on with no great success. The rice grains stuck to each other like long-lost brothers, the puris refused to swell with pride and the custard was a grim, lumped clod.

The only thing that came out with flying colours and tasted 'just like Mom makes it' was the tomato chutney. Glistening red, with plump brown raisins swimming gloriously, it was a sight to behold. It had just that right amount of sweet, salt and tang. I was so proud of it!

Our guests arrived, pleasantries were exchanged and we finally gravitated towards the food that I had laid out. Our friends ploughed through my casualties. It must have been an ordeal for them but to my great surprise, the food was almost over. They helped me to clean up and after a few more minutes of chatting, said their farewells.

As I headed back to my room, past the dining table, I noticed a bowl standing forlorn at the far corner of the table. I peeped into it and there, in all its pristine glory, stood the one saving grace of the evening — the delicious tomato chutney — unnoticed, untouched and untasted!

Mita Banerjee

9

THE IN-LAWS

Remember that happiness is a way of travel, not a destination.

–Roy Goodman

Mother-in-Law and I

It was the summer of 2005 (May, perhaps) when her parents came home. I can't forget the day because the moment Ms Shantha stepped into our house, she said: 'Kinda stuffy in here, isn't it?'

Mr Chandran knew I had overheard it and thus kept mum. He would continue to keep mum on many more such occasions.

Ms Shantha's next statement (which thankfully my parents didn't hear) was: 'Kind of dark, aren't they?'

Like I said, Mr Chandran kept mum.

If my mother-in-law was a fat person, distracting her would have been a piece of cake — yeah literally, I only had to offer her a piece of cake and she would have busied herself in eating. But she wasn't fat, so I couldn't do anything while she continued to insult me and my ancestors.

Thankfully, we Rajans know how to fight from the trenches... And I asked my parents to do just that. Everything went well and it was decided that on 8 September 2005, Rekha and I will get married at a temple in Cherrukunnu, Kannur, Kerala. I was a little upset as I didn't expect my mother-in-law to be such a problem. I was under the impression that I will sweep her off her feet with my sense of humour. But that was not to be.

As luck would have it, Rekha and I didn't enter into a major fight before 8 September 2005 and the marriage happened as scheduled.

Marriage over. All relatives gone.

Rekha and I hired a cab to Kumarakom for our honeymoon. I was still reeling under the insults from my mother-in-law. At least, outlaws are wanted… What was one to do with in-laws?

I blurted out: 'Rekha, don't you think your mom talks too much?'

'What? Haven't you heard your mom talking?'

This was enough to ensure that the next two hours were silent. If you don't know how difficult it is for a man on his way to his honeymoon to keep silent for two hours, try it when you get married. We still had three hours of the journey left, so I tried to break the silence using my self-acclaimed excellent sense of humour. I pointed at some sheep grazing in the fields by the roadside and said: 'Relatives of yours?'

Rekha didn't even look up. She just said: 'Yes. Remember, I just got married? They are my new in-laws!'

I didn't try to patch up till we reached Kumarakom. When we were half way into our honeymoon, we became friends again.

Jamshed Velayuda Rajan

My Wife and Her Mother-in-Law

Something happened two months ago that brought about radical changes in my daily life. I got married! Since then, I have been caught in a peculiar form of tug-of-war between my wife and my mother.

Every time they fight, I get calls of enquiry from them, to find out the time I would be getting back home from work. Armed with the knowledge that the evening would be stressful and long, I ensure a late arrival.

If my mother opens the door for me, my wife will be at an arm's distance to grab my laptop bag. If my wife brings me the towel and asks me to freshen up quickly, my mother insists that I relax and drink a glass of lemonade.

I look at my father for support but he stays conveniently hidden behind his newspaper, or simply shrugs his shoulders and continues watching the television. This action clearly conveys the message that, 'Buddy, I've had my share, it is your turn now!'

At the dinner table, the conversation is minimal. The long gaps of silence are filled with the friction of utensils which are a lot noisier than normal days. The decibel levels indicate the magnitude of the fight.

If my wife asks me how my day was, I reply casually that it was fine. If I said that my day was great, she would break into a bout of self-pity, making the fight even more difficult to resolve.

My mother then rephrases the question and asks me the same thing again, trying to prove that her son is more responsive to her. So I just play safe and say, 'It was okay.'

As my wife is a Malayali, my mother starts conversing in Tamil, but I ensure that I respond in a neutral language, lest my wife thinks we were conspiring against her.

I look at my father again, but that intelligent man buries his face in his plate and concentrates on the food as if it was his newspaper.

After dinner, my mother tries to prolong my stay outside the bedroom by offering ice-cream, fruits and even chyawanprash. If I indulge in these after-dinner activities, my wife makes statements like, 'I am sleepy' or 'Don't you want to come and watch your favourite television show'? Not wanting to upset either of them, I take a spoon full of chyawanprash and rush to the bedroom.

Once inside the room, I stare at the television as my wife sits before the dressing mirror and sulks until I am forced to ask, 'What happened, honey?'

Even before I finish my question, she starts crying and explains how my mother is actually a witch, and that both my father and I have not realised this in the last thirty years, but she has, in just two months.

I console her by saying that my mother needs to be

controlled with an iron hand. My wife is happy and we both sleep peacefully.

The next day while wearing my shoes, I ask my mother which colour socks would look better.

My mother says, 'The black one.'

I dump the blue socks and wear the black one, as my mother suggests. On my way out, I whisper into her ears: 'I know you guys fought last evening. But I trust you... Even before wearing my socks, I consult you.' She smiles gleefully.

As I start the car, I peep into the rear view mirror only to see my wife bringing in two cups of tea to the balcony. She and my mother then sit on the cane chairs and chat happily as if nothing ever happened. Until the next time when something does happen... They really do like each other!

Jamshed Velayuda Rajan

Not My Loss

Pleasant memories leave a lasting impression on our minds but the unpleasant ones etch a scar on the soul.

After five months of our marriage, I was visiting my in-laws' house for the first time. Just like any other bride, I was anxious to meet my husband's family but I was apprehensive about the unpleasant circumstances. We had got married against the wishes of my mother-in-law and she had severed all ties with us. This is not how we wanted it to be and decided to take the first step towards restoring harmonious relations with her.

Two days later, we boarded the train to Pune. I stepped in, not daring to look back, lest I had a change of mind and jumped off the train. As the train chugged to a start, I wished I could just keep travelling forever and never reach my destination. I had a sinking feeling and my mind kept wandering until I fell asleep.

'Chai...garam chai...' I woke up to the sound of hawkers selling tea. It was six a.m. In another hour, we would be there. I tried to divert my mind by chatting with a co-passenger. Soon, the train stopped at the Pune station. It was time to say a small prayer before getting off.

Within the next fifteen minutes, our cab pulled up outside the house. As soon as we stepped inside the gate, we heard sounds of sobbing coming from inside. My feet froze and my heart skipped a beat.

My mother-in-law stood at the threshold of the house with puffed-up eyes. It was she who had been crying! I was confused and disheartened. Wasn't she supposed to express joy when a bride came home for the first time? I bowed down and touched her feet but there was no response. Suddenly, a maid came forward with mustard seeds and red chilly in her hands, circled it over our heads and threw it behind us. We were taken aback. This was a ritual that is traditionally performed by the groom's mother.

There was a cold spell of silence as she escorted me to my room and went away. I sat on the bed, hurt and humiliated. My husband entered the room and sat down beside me. He gently held my hands and said, 'Give her some time, everything will be alright.'

'What if she never accepts me?'

'That would be her loss, not yours, right?'

At that moment, all my worries evaporated. I forgot that I was a daughter-in-law. I was simply my wonderful husband's bride and the only thing that mattered to me was the intense look of love in his eyes that healed my bruises before they could leave scars on my soul.

There was one thing I decided then and there though! If I have a son and he decides to marry the girl of his choice, I would definitely give his bride a warm welcome, even if I did not like her.

Mira Pawar

Runaway Bride

I had never really cared much about marriage. Honestly. Now, I am not saying that I am in some evolved place where women are far superior to men, though on second thoughts, that may be so! And why not? We can MULTITASK! Do you know of any man who can?

Wait, this is not what I started to write about. Let me get back on track. So, as I was saying, while growing up I had not thought much about marriage. I did not dream about a prince on a white horse galloping over to save me from the demons! I did not want to be swept off my feet by the tall dark stranger! So when at the age of twenty-five, I met Sridhar, he just seemed like a nice guy! We met over the holi weekend that year at the home of mutual friends. I remember thinking that it was so good to meet someone with whom one did not have to put on an act. Sridhar was so easy to be with, so easy to swap life stories with. He made me laugh. I think that's what I liked about him best. So there I was, a typical, if a little cynical, woman in Mumbai spending the weekend with my future husband and falling so in love that I was ready to fight any demon myself. Little did I know that the demons would come in the form of my in-laws!

Sridhar belonged to an ultra conservative Andhra family governed by a mother whose ambition in life was to get him married to the incarnation of sati-savitri herself! She was looking for a 'beautiful, fair, slim, tall, well mannered, obedient and rich-with-dowry' daughter-in-law and her son went ahead and proposed to me. Not only did I not fit her idea of a perfect bahu, I also did not care two hoots for it. In Sridhar I found a friend and did not care to worship him. What he saw in me remains a mystery to this day!

After about a year of struggling with a long-distance relationship, I decided to move to Bangalore to be with the man I had decided to marry. At this stage in a couple's life, the soon-to-be in-laws are introduced and thus started the most painful period of my life. Even though my parents took the news of an inter-community marriage hard, their attempt to 'reason' with me ended when they met Sridhar. Alas, my meeting with my mother-in-law was a disaster. She tried her best to disillusion me to the extent of showing me pictures of Sridhar with his ex-girlfriend. What she tried to achieve is anyone's guess.

So there we were, very convinced that we were meant to be together, and the negative forces of family only added to our determination. It didn't take us long to realise that we would never get the blessings of my in-laws, so we decided to deal with that later and get married first. It was not an easy decision, especially for Sridhar, but it seemed that we had no choice. We had two choices: give in to parental pressure or make our own decision. We decided to elope.

At first we decided to leave both sets of parents out of it but by that time my parents had taken a fondness to Sridhar and wanted to be a part of our marriage ceremony, so we decided to marry at my parents' place in my hometown. It was a semi-elopement so to say. And thus started the planning for a wedding, part-celebration part-secret

I don't know what was most exciting about the day. The fact that I was the centre of attention for everyone or the fact that some 1000 kms away there was a family who had no idea that I was becoming a part of theirs. Sridhar arrived with a band of his friends in full secrecy. Keeping with the theme, none of his friends had informed their families as to where they were headed! It was hilarious.

And so, we were married with the blessings of my family but away from his. When at last Sridhar announced at home that he had gone ahead and married me, all hell broke loose. His mother kept sending messages of ill health and doom. But even under such reactions, we were happy.

It's been seven years now and we are still happy. His parents live with us now and that has worked out well too. I don't know whether we did the right thing but I do know that if we had not gotten married the way we did, we would never have ended up together. All's well that ends well, right!

Amrita Srinivasan

The Braided Bride

The boy's mother goes through the entire hassle of bearing and rearing a son, inspecting and rejecting scores of matches for him before she finds that perfect mix of culinary ability, tolerable beauty and docility she approves of. And so it is only fair for her to be the uncrowned queen at her son's wedding.

My cousin was marrying the boy who had chased her till she consented. This was of course a major setback to the boy's mother, who thought she should have been doing the chasing. But her twenty-five year old love-stricken, independent-minded and well-settled boy obviously had a mind of his own.

The girl wasn't bad to look at. She could cook, clean, sing a bit and even belonged to the same caste. Even though she was rather strong-willed and not the docile mouse who is such a joy to mothers-in-law, there was no reason to disapprove of her as a daughter-in-law. But there is something called an ego.

There had to be some reason to object. Hopefully, by the wedding day there would be one.

There was. On the left side of the hall, there was a large group of relatives from the groom's side and a matching army from the bride's side, on the right. The women on the girl's side wore their hair in long braids, decorated with gold and silver strands called kunjalams. The women on the boy's side wore their hair in a bun, covered with lots of jasmine flowers. There was no other difference — everyone was slapping Chennai's giant mosquitoes, sweating in their Kancheepuram silks and complaining about the agninakshatram, Chennai's peak summer period. They kept crowding the dining hall, eating vast quantities of breakfast, lunch and dinner at the bride's brothers' expense.

As the mother-in-law walked around attending to her guests, she overheard a conversation.

'It's lucky that the shubha muhurtham is late in the morning. We can dress up the bride beautifully. Our girl is very beautiful, with hair that goes down to her knees. She has half the hair in the family, you know.'

'Oh, yes! I had peeped into the dressing room. She's got a lovely jadai, with lots of flowers and a gold kunjalam.'

Ah… Finally! It was the music she had waited for. What a delicious reason to create a fuss! A queen could reign, even if she doesn't rule. She barged into the dressing room.

My cousin's hair had been oiled generously with coconut oil till it shone as brightly as a bulb. She had combed it several times to remove all the tangles. The stylist had then split it into three parts and pleated it, using a string of jasmine flowers as the fourth strand. It was finished with a very pretty kunjalam that had gold and silver threads. That is the style we Tamils call a jadai.

'Oh! namaskaram, Auntie. I am the bride's cousin, and I am helping her dress. Isn't she looking as beautiful as Goddess Meenakshi herself?'

'Umm… Yes. Very nice, but you have to undo the jadai and bun it up into a kondai with a coil of jasmine flowers around it. In our tradition, the bride must be made to look like Devi Andal.'

Everyone was paralyzed with shock.

'Auntie, we have taken two hours to prepare the jadai. How can we change it now when there is less than half-an-hour before the priest calls her?'

'All that is fine, but in our district, the bride always wears a kondai. I want my bride to wear one, too. You may think we use one bottle of coconut oil for the whole year, but you need to understand our tradition. She will be a part of our family after all.'

'But, Auntie...'

'No buts. I have brought lots of fresh jasmine flowers. Quickly, redo the hairstyle.'

There was obviously no way to stop the wedding, but she could at least bring in a dramatic pause. There had to be something to savour after she had retired and the daughter-in-law had taken over the house.

The two sides plunged into battle with gusto. The women on the bride's side pleaded to be allowed to follow their will, since the girl was not yet married. After the wedding they could make her follow all their traditions. The women on the groom's side insisted that it was a matter of prestige. Everyone had followed this custom, and they would not compromise just because this girl was from another district.

The girl's father, the boy's father and the priest were called. They refused to intervene in a 'women's dispute'. The boy was called. He was asked whether his mother and motherland were at all important to him. He looked around helplessly. There was no answer that could satisfy everybody. Should he please his mother or his wife-to-be? Was she going to be his wife now?

He tried to look at her. She was somewhere in the room, near the mirror, but his vision was blocked by the two Kancheepuram-clad brigades.

He mustered some courage and announced, 'I think the decision lies in the hands of the bride since it is her special day!' The women from the boy's side looked aghast. The brigades parted and the groom held his breath as the bride emerged.

The jadai had been undone and the bride winked secretly at her groom while coiling flowers around the kondai she had made.

The groom heaved a sigh of relief. The queen smiled. The day she had waited for had finally come.

Raamesh Gowri Raghavan

The Centre Piece

Ashish squeezed my hand comfortingly as our car stopped outside my new home. 'Weeping brides are passé,' he whispered in my ears and I smiled.

In keeping with the tradition, my mother-in-law had come home from the wedding before us, to welcome her son and daughter-in-law into the house, as a couple, for the first time. She was supposed to be waiting at the door with the ceremonial thali. The minutes ticked away, but she was nowhere to be seen. A few moments later, a sleepy mother in-law came stumbling out and raced through the rituals with a forced smile pasted on her face.

Sitting in 'my room', I was anxious to take a bath after which I would be able to get some sleep. I waited for the giggling female relatives to leave the room, who were mesmerised by my lehnga, which was indeed magnificent, besides being extremely heavy and stifling. I excused myself into the bathroom and freshened up. I stepped back into the room only to find my mother-in-law sitting in the centre of the bed. She asked me to get some rest. It took me a while to realise that she was determined to guard me while I slept. This was the time when Ashish would come to 'our room' and she would finally have to surrender her only son to 'the girl from outside'!

Some sympathetic relatives kept trying to draw her out of the room for various reasons, but she was more than a match for them. Each time Ashish entered the room to rest, she would ask him to go and sleep elsewhere. After five abortive attempts to lie down in his own room, Ashish finally turned to leave, when an uncle pushed him right back in.

I was just wondering what would happen next, when she yawned widely: 'I am sooo... sleepy,' she murmured, and lay down in the middle of our bed and promptly went to sleep! Ashish and I stared at her in shock! Looking at each other, we burst into giggles at the absurdity of it all. We decided to grab some much needed sleep — with our hands interlocked above my oblivious mother-in-law's head. Of course, we would let go hurriedly each time she stirred.

Ever since, Ashish and I have worked out our equilibrium. We manage to largely ignore her frenzied behaviour and lead a fulfilling life as she continues her fruitless attempts at trying to be the centre piece in our lives!

Parul Gupta

The Green Streak

'How can she give THE BLUE CAR to Shakku bai, the maid?'

'We had bought it for Yash from Europe when he was eleven, and it's his favourite car!'

'He has treasured it since that day and not let it out of his room, and it's been only a month since Radhika has come into his life and she is emptying out his treasures.'

Manjala was filled with fury when she told this to Mukesh in a soft voice so that Radhika would not hear her.

Yash and Radhika had been married a month ago and the problems had already started. Manjala was not able to adapt herself to Radhika's ways. Yash being the first child had always been Manjala's favourite, she had pampered him unconditionally and had received equal attention back from Yash, and now she was unable to share his love with Radhika.

She had not realised that the green streak of jealousy was striking her. She assumed it was all Radhika's fault.

Mukesh, Manjala's husband, had been listening to her for a while now. Last week she had told him about the bundle of clothes which Radhika had removed from Yash's cupboard, which Neelie, their daughter, had sent, also instructing the chef about the cooking, making changes in Yash's bedroom and a few more things which he was unable to recollect.

Now before things got out of hand, he needed to get control of the whole situation. He made Manjala sit with him and asked her what the problem was. Why was she keeping a watch on Radhika's actions, whether she removed 'the blue car', Yash's old clothes which his sister had sent for him a year ago, or whether it was telling the chef about Yash's likes and dislikes.

Manjala sat back and said, 'She knows Yash for only a month now and I have known him for the past twenty-eight years. How can she decide what he would like to eat for lunch or breakfast? I can't let her have control over him entirely, he is my son and if I let go so easily, then she will make him dance to her tunes.'

Mukesh was shocked to hear her speak so; he had never seen Manjala speak in this tone. Manjala meant 'sweet voice', and she had always kept up to the meaning of her name but today she was different. He could sense she had become extremely possessive about Yash and was not ready to let go of him or his things.

Mukesh spoke after a silence, he was getting angry but he knew he wouldn't be able to get his way out with anger so he spoke softly. 'What do you mean when you say about controlling Yash? He is no child, and he need not be controlled by either of you. He has a mind of his own, and if Radhika has removed his old stuff, what is all the hue and cry about? Yash cannot stick to his old things forever, and I am sure it's not Yash who is having the problem but it's you who is not able to accept it.'

He continued when he realised she was giving thought to what he was saying. 'You have been ruling this house for so many years, your insecurities are not letting you accept a new person in the house, she is the new bride and instead of helping her adjust, you are being a hindrance in her path.'

He spoke, this time with a little more emphasis. 'Manjala, when you got married, Amma had been so kind to you, she had immediately given you the keys to the whole house, she treated you like a queen, how can you forget that? Now, when you have got the opportunity to be in her shoes, you are simply digging your heels in! Radhika belongs to the new generation and is an open minded girl, a little bit of love and you will win her heart.'

He added, 'You can share the same relationship with her as you share with Neelie, and you have been missing Neelie since she has shifted to Manchester.'

Manjala thought about what Mukesh was saying and knew he was right. Why was she behaving in this manner? She didn't want to be like a typical Indian woman who was scared her son would run away with his wife and in her old age she would be alone. She had never cared about such things. She had enough bank balance of her own to bother about such a trivial thing but even then, this she had not done justice to Radhika and had tethered herself to Yash.

She had made up her mind to be more accepting and an opportunity turned up soon enough.

It was Yash's birthday. Manjala made kheer for him, his favourite dish since childhood. Radhika had, however, prepared an elaborate Italian dinner: pastas, salad, lasagna. Manjala looked at her pale kheer and wondered at the fate of that small dish in front of the chic cuisine. But she quickly shooed away the feeling and told herself that even if he didn't relish it, it would be okay, most of the younger generation preferred Italian anyway. She did not enter the kitchen to make sure the kheer was served. She left it to Radhika.

Radhika placed the kheer in a silver bowl right along with the pasta and she helped herself to a generous portion too. Manjala could only smile as she saw her son ravishing it all with equal delight.

There never was really any competition, it was only in her mind!

Mukesh, who was watching all of this from a quiet corner, smiled to himself. He knew his Manjala had become the 'sweet voice' she was known for and the green-eyed ghoul had finally left her...

Aarti Sonthalia

10

WELCOME TO THE FAMILY

Other things may change us, but we start and end with family.

–Anthony Brandt

An Air Force Bride

When one married a man in uniform, one wheeled off by train to remote places like Chabua, Hashimara, Izzatnagar, Avantipur, Uttarlai... Some names not even mentioned on any but the most detailed maps. So it was with me. I left Mumbai, where I was born and educated, for Hindon, in UP, in the heat of summer. I had heard stories of how young couples (the new bride, mainly) were welcomed at stations (both railway and Air Force) by squadron-mates, their families and their pets. The cheapest band available in the closest village was employed to belch out-of-tune, screechy Hindi film songs. Cars were rare then so a military truck or a rickshaw (cycle or motorised) was decorated with colourful paper streamers, some balloons, to transport the couple 'home'. Either everyone squeezed into the same vehicle, or it was escorted by a bevy of motorcycles through the long drive (camps were always several kilometers away from town).

Sometimes, if the squadron was flying at the time of arrival, an aircraft or two flew over the station and the bride was welcomed by wings dipped from side to side in a 'salute'.

One story I heard was about brother officers of the groom who dressed up as daakoos and pretended to want to kidnap the bride on arrival. The newly-married husband put up a vigorous fight and actually injured one before they gave up their masks and declared their real identities. Then there were the bedroom stories of how people didn't allow the couple to sleep at all or pinned condoms to the sheets.

I was a civilian bride, with no clue of military traditions, no knowledge of what life in Camp entailed, no exposure to rural India, no awareness of anything outside Bombay ('Mumbai' was two decades away). I probably knew more about New York than neighbouring Nashik, though I hadn't visited either place. STD booths were just springing up, televisions were not rare, but still confined to the upper classes. The fact that I was permanently going to set up home in a strangely named place invited OMG gasps from all I knew.

The thirty-six hour train journey across India, across so many geographic boundaries, so many different terrains, was an education in itself. As expected, my husband's colleagues were there to receive us at the station with a huge, brown, net-covered, monster-truck with massive wheels. My seat had been reserved at one end of the un-cushioned metal bench that ran along the truck's inside 'wall'. The indication that it was mine was a cardboard heart with my name on it, garishly pink and pasted with sprigs of fresh leaves and some rosebuds. A special pillow had been tied to the bench for my comfort, may I add. A convoy of friends and colleagues on motorcycles honked alongside as we bumped over the kutccha roads to Camp.

My first view of unbelievable neatness and tidiness. All those same-looking houses, no garbage, no traffic, no beggars, did seem like a different world, all those tended gardens, the huge shady flowering trees in full summer bloom, the birds, the shiny insects, the clear blue sky, healthy people riding by on cycles, with children and wives perched on the front-bar and at the back, too, and shopping bags dangling from the handles… First impressions of what I would enjoy for years to come. There were no religious rituals, no tikka, no aarti, just the warm earth below me, the fresh flora around, smiles flashing here, there, everywhere, and the heavens above. Wow!

My life's possessions fitted into one trunk. As I was later to discover, my husband's possessions fitted into another. Inclusive of kitchen things, may I add, for we owned neither gas nor fridge, cutlery nor crockery, nor any curios. Only linen, clothes and some books.

We were taken to his Flight Commander's house as shortage of quarters meant couples like us had to wait for many months before we got even temporary accommodation. I learnt overnight that I'd have to play musical-houses like the other couples. Whoever went on leave left their keys behind so homeless creatures like us could occupy that abode till they returned.

I knew nil cooking. Indeed, I couldn't even identify one dal from another. I was shopping challenged. I didn't know how to spend money; I'd never done that before, other than pay for my fees and my train pass. I didn't know what to do with the vegetables I'd bought. Bless those senior wives and super neighbours (too many to mention). They taught me survival skills in my borrowed kitchens, in their own kitchens, by word of mouth, through pressure-cooker recipe books and most delightful of all, by inviting me over for innumerable laughter-filled lunches and dinners. Besides the basic poha and upma, I made pineapple upside-down cakes and stuffed putti samosas. I learnt to make khichdi and to make biryani. I learnt from everyone! My part-time maid kneaded flour in the milk-vessel to use every bit of nutrition and to make the cleaning easier. My dhobhi taught me to make good starch with rice-water: mix it with arrow-root powder, he advised. The Mess cook taught me how to make a disastrous pudding good just by rearranging and garnishing it properly. Of course, I was forgiven all mistakes. I was young, I had to be forgiven. I learnt that a single wick stove with a beer-bottle full of kerosene could make lunch for four people, that petrol was not a substitute for kerosene, that it was dangerous to check the temperature of water when a home-made heater (a length of naked metal spring wound around a wooden stick, balanced at the edge of a bucket upon a bent hanger) was dunked in it. And that life without a fridge was possible.

Indeed, coming from Bombay, I couldn't have imagined a life without electricity, and I discovered that that could be fun if managed properly. What's more, I got to sleep under the stars at night, my man and I together, separated from the universe by a mosquito net.

I learnt about the birds and the bees first hand, of course, but also through naughty jokes, gently cracked through games. My hysterical giggles became a legend.

There was no public transport. If I wanted to go somewhere, I walked. When we could afford a cycle, I pedalled. Not a bad deal, considering I saw on the way to the market Saras cranes, peacocks, a mongoose or two hundreds babblers, squirrels, and flowering shrubs in season: perks no one advertises that more than make up for the lack of urban amenities!

I was pampered as the youngest member of the Squadron till another bride came in and took my place. But those memories, ah... They are forever.

Sheela Jaywant

Different Strokes

'Sardar and Mrs Charanjit Singh Kapoor invite you to the marriage of their granddaughter Simran to Anoop, Son of Mr and Mrs Thomas Varkey'

The cards had been sent out and Simran was furious. Nothing was going right. 'He printed "marriage" instead of "wedding"! How could he, after the number of times I explained it to him?' Simran wailed.

'Get over it!' her mother chided. With a week to go for the wedding, and a million things that should have been done yesterday, the printing error was the last thing on her mind. The last six months had been a roller coaster ride, and she was still on it!

When Anoop, a true Syrian Catholic Christian from Kerala met Simran, a spirited PR consultant from a Sikh family in Delhi, they hit it off immediately. A torrid romance followed and they decided to get married.

When Anoop broke the news to his family, there was pandemonium.

'She won't understand our culture; she doesn't even know

our language!' his mother objected. 'Think about your poor mother. Who will marry your sister?' his aunt added.

Anoop was having none of it. 'It's her or no one,' he said adamantly.

The next few months were stressful for Simran. Caught between love for his girlfriend and mother, Anoop had become withdrawn. His behaviour was curt and at times he was even rude. Simran was not sure if she could take it any longer.

Eventually, Anoop's mother relented with the condition that the wedding would be held in Kerala, at the family church, complete with all paraphernalia of a Syrian Catholic wedding. Simran's family agreed. They were willing to do anything for their daughter's happiness.

Simran could not get over her apprehensions. 'Will I be able to adjust with the family? They have been so hostile. How can I ignore that? Will they overcome their prejudices?' she fretted.

Coming from a typical Punjabi family, the tenets of a Malyali wedding were alien to Simran. Things came to a head when she learnt that the ceremony would be conducted in Malyalam.

'I guess I just have to be present for my wedding, right? I won't even understand anything but you don't care, do you?' she screamed at him.

'Think as you please, I have other things to worry about right now,' he retorted.

Simran put the phone down and wondered if she was doing the right thing by marrying Anoop. Maybe it was a bad decision, but she loved him too much, and both had been through a lot. She prayed for courage.

The Kapoor family landed in Kochi and were welcomed by torrential showers. Simran wondered if it was an omen.

The day of the wedding was dark and cloudy. Simran looked at the weather and then at her heavy bridal sari. This is not how she had imagined her wedding day to be. Anoop and his family's behaviour made her feel lonely and depressed. Gulping down her tears, she started getting ready.

During the hour-long drive to the church, Simran had butterflies in her tummy. They reached the church to find Anoop and his family waiting for them. Her groom looked dapper in a summer suit. The church looked magnificent. As they walked inside, the choir struck a beautiful melody and she was enchanted by the music.

At the altar, the priest welcomed the congregation and announced, 'Today's ceremony will be conducted in English for the benefit of the bride and her family.' Simran's face lit up with joy and she looked at Anoop. He smiled and winked at her.

Suddenly, the clouds vanished and rays of the brightly shining sun streamed in through the large windows. It was a beautiful day and a moving ceremony.

They were finally married. As they drove down to Anoop's house, her apprehensions crept back again.

The car pulled up in the driveway and she saw her mother-in-law standing at the threshold with a reassuring smile on her face. At the entrance, everybody chanted a prayer and a rosary along with a lighted candle was given to her.

'What do I do now?' the young bride panicked and looked at her husband for help.

There was a gentle touch on her elbow. It was her mother-in-law. 'Walk into the house, one step at a time, and every time with the right foot. I was here at the same place twenty-five years ago, feeling the same way. But don't worry; I will take good care of you. Welcome home, *mole* (daughter)!'

Simran was overwhelmed. At that moment, it made no difference that she did not know their language, rituals and customs. She was simply a young bride making her way in to a new home and a new life... And she was definitely not alone!

Prerna Uppal

Halwa

It was love at first sight when I set my eyes upon Sammy at the traditional dikhai, where the boy and girl meet under the strict supervision of their parents.

Within a month, we were married and I was looking forward to spending time with my new husband. For the first few months, we went to live in Sammy's ancestral home in a small town with his parents, who wanted me to get acquainted with their lifestyle before we moved to a different city.

The house was teeming with relatives who had loud voices and raucous laughter. I was horrified and consoled myself that it was not going to be this way forever. Sammy, I and innumerable other people always had all our meals together, which was a rather noisy and frenzied affair. I was happy just squeezing Sammy's hand under the table. It was only Sammy who mattered to me. Breakfast was followed by a lavish lunch. Then there was tea with samosas or some fried savouries from the market, and the day ended with a huge dinner.

The women sat around discussing recipes, laughing, gossiping and showing their new clothes and jewellery to each other. The men discussed politics, recession and the stock exchange. The conversations were endless and the constant commotion jarred my nerves.

Sammy was the youngest and shared a warm companionship with his cousins. I never tried to be a part of it. The atmosphere was overwhelming and I craved for moments alone with Sammy.

One day, Sammy's mother informed me that I would have to prepare a sweet dish for the entire family. It was a tradition. I was shocked as I had never cooked before, and to do it for the first time for a hundred eyes and fifty mouths was terrifying.

I entered the kitchen and stared blankly at the utensils. I was obviously going to make a fool of myself. Just then Sammy's aunt walked in. With a reassuring look, she poured some ghee into a vessel, handed me a karchi and asked me to just keep stirring. She added flour, sugar, milk and nuts, and soon the halwa was ready. It smelt delicious.

'The new bahu has made halwa,' she screamed in her loudest voice. The halwa was first given as bhog (offering) to our temple deity and then served to the elders of the family. Everyone praised it and gave me token money as their blessings.

I had done nothing. Some other women of the house were aware of this too, as they had been peeping occasionally into the kitchen. But no one said anything except commend my efforts. Sammy came in smiling with pride.

'See we found the perfect wife for you, didn't we?' his mother and aunt teased him.

'Yes,' Sammy laughed.

I felt guilty about my uncaring approach to the family; for not even trying to be a part of them. Everything felt different now. I still squeezed Sammy's hand under the table, but was also a keen participant in the family's conversations and their lives.

As told to Anu Chopra

Over the Threshold

I couldn't believe what was happening! It was my wedding day, and instead of being on cloud nine, I was distressed. I could hear murmurs around me, some sympathetic and reassuring, others harsh and scornful. The passing doctors and nurses stared at me in my bridal finery. Looking down at the still face of my father-in-law, I prayed to God to help us out of this calamity.

Like any other dreamy-eyed bride, I was looking forward to my new life with excitement. Our house had come alive with joy. There was chaos amidst enthusiasm as I was being dressed up in the traditional Kerala bridal attire, an off-white and gold mundu-veshti. A few strands of jasmine flowers in my hair completed the picture. We were one of the few families who believed in simplicity, and I was lucky to be marrying into a family with similar beliefs.

Ours has been a beautiful love story. We had grown up together and were unprepared when cupid struck. Despite his deep feelings for me, the Capricornian trait compelled him to disguise his emotions. When he did finally bare his heart to me, I smiled and acted coy instead of fainting in his arms. I was thrilled to be marrying my best friend!

Loud sobs from my mother-in-law jerked me back to the present. My husband and his brother looked shaken up. After the wedding ceremony, my father-in-law had suddenly collapsed. There was a moment of horrified silence before my doctor aunt took over and immediately whisked him off to the hospital. I was in a state of utter disbelief. I had hardly stepped into their lives and misfortune struck. There were all kinds of assumptions... The heat, stress, lack of sleep or ME! Even in the twenty-first century, people clung on to superstitious beliefs, accusing individuals for no valid reason.

Here I was, waiting with bated breath for the doctor's diagnosis when my mother-in-law's eyes fell on my tearful face. She walked up to me, hugged me tightly and said, 'What has to be will be. There is someone up there pulling the strings. I leave everything in His capable hands.' Having uttered these words, she asked her elder son to take care of the situation in the hospital, as she had to take her daughter-in-law home for the first time. She believed in the rahu kaalam (auspicious time) and we had to leave immediately. Everybody around was taken aback by her strength and self-control.

Once we reached home, I got ready to step over the threshold when she gently stopped me. Wiping my tears she said, 'You are the Lakshmi of this house; enter with a smile on your face. Welcome into our home, my dearest daughter, for that is what you will be to me always. Daughters bring good fortune and that is what you should always believe.' She did not know that she had lifted a huge weight off my heart.

When I hear of brides being burnt and tortured for no fault of theirs, I wish every girl could have a mother-in-law like mine; that way the world would be a better place. I have been married for seventeen years and every moment has been special, enriched by the warm presence of my parents-in-law.

Neelima Varma

Surprise Gifts

Once a girl is of 'marriageable age', everyone around her makes a worthy note of it. It was time for Ishita, too, to tie the knot.

After her twenty-fourth birthday, her parents filtered out candidates and arranged for meetings with 'suitable grooms'. She met each one with an open mind, but none of them stirred her interest.

One day, her parents informed her about a boy called Avishek. The two families had spoken and mutually agreed to let Ishita and Avishek decide if they wanted to have a future together.

A chain of phone calls started and in a couple of days, the two youngsters had a fair idea about each other. They liked each other and had even exchanged cards and small gifts, but Avishek never brought up the topic of marriage.

Ishita was informed by her office that she would have to leave for Australia on an assignment, for a month. By that time she knew that she was in love with Avishek and hoped this would rouse him to move a step ahead in their relationship. Nothing happened. Ishita was disappointed as she hugged him goodbye at the airport.

A week after she reached Australia, she received a parcel. The handwriting on the parcel was Avishek's. He had doodled his trademark 'smiley' on it, just as he did in all his cards. Ishita was thrilled and nervous as she tore open the wrapper. What she saw inside blew her away. It was not a gift from Avishek!

The package contained a beautiful red and gold sari with a note that read:

Priyo Ishita,

Ami tomay nijer meyer moto pochhondo kori.

asha kori ei sari ta tomar pochhondo hobe.

Iti,

Ma

(Dear Ishita, I love you like my daughter. I hope you will like this sari. Regards, Ma)

Ishita could not believe her eyes. It was a big surprise and a warm expression of love and acceptance. The sari, fit for a bride, was symbolic of a formal marriage proposal sealed and stamped (with the smiley) by Avishek himself!

Ishita did not know how to react to this beautiful gesture. She was at a loss for words and overjoyed at such a hearty welcome into a new family.

The engagement was finalised for the day after Ishita returned to India. On the day of the ceremony, when she arrived looking gorgeous in the red and gold sari, she noticed Avishek looking stunned and her mother-in-law secretly wiping a tear from the corner of her eye.

Mudra Kirtibhai Rawal

The Firangi Bride

'My son is marrying a firangi girl who will be living with us in the same house,' bawled Alpona. She was desperate for sympathy from her friends who squealed with joy in unison. The thought of a tall, slim, white, liberated woman falling in love with their Ajoy was exhilarating. This reaction was in stark contrast to what Alpona had expected from her orthodox, starched-cotton-saree-clad friends.

We lived in a joint family and everybody was actually looking forward to the wedding. It would be fun to have a foreigner amongst us. Alpona felt betrayed. Her imagination ran wild as she grumbled untiringly. What would happen to her Lakshmi pujas on Thursdays and Shani pujas on Saturdays? The firangi bride would play havoc with her holy menus on those days.

Alpona was up at 6 a.m. and walked dizzily up and down her verandah. Her son would be here with his bride very soon. The flimsy fabric of her chiffon saree accentuated the rounded contours of her huge body and kept slipping off her shoulders. 'What happened to the beautiful Bengal cotton sarees that you usually wear? Oh God! You are wearing pencil heels!' quipped Dipankar, amused at his wife's peculiar appearance. Alpona glared at him.

The sound of a car pulling up quickened her pulse. 'Hurry, put on the Ma Kali kirtan cassette,' she ordered her husband. 'Where is my puja plate? I must welcome her in our traditional way with the lighted lamp. That will put her in place right from the moment she enters our house. No Western lifestyle here,' she said as Dipankar suppressed a chuckle.

Ajoy emerged with Olga from the taxi. Alpona noticed her lovely long hair with grudging admiration. She pushed her cheek forward to be kissed but Olga joined her palms together and said 'Namaste', stunning everyone with her sincere effort. Alpona welcomed the bride with a heavy heart.

There were numerous phone calls from curious relatives and Alpona had the same conversation with all of them, 'Olga is so beaoootiphoool. We are having our typical Indian cardamom tea and she loves it.' We were amused at her sudden burst of English.

The atmosphere at home was lively and Alpona had consoled herself by giving this marriage an expiry date of one year.

Olga made a dazzling Bengali bride. Her white, glowing face offset the magenta Benarasi saree, and her hair was tied up in a bun embellished with golden brooches. Dots of sandalwood paste decorated her forehead. Her kohl-lined eyes sparkled with joy. Ajoy stood elegant and handsome next to her in his dhoti and silk shawl.

'Our wedding rituals are elaborate and tedious,' Alpona warned Olga sadistically.

'Ma, this will be the most beautiful experience of my life and I can hardly wait for the ceremony,' gushed Olga. Alpona smiled to herself. She probably visualised the poor girl sweating in the blaze of the fire and the smoke. To her disappointment, Olga sailed through the long rituals happily.

Six months passed. Alpona was over the phone, declaring to a friend that the time may have come. Olga had been crying. She and Ajoy had probably quarrelled. No sooner had she hung up that we saw Ajoy escorting Olga out with his arms protectively draped around her, disappointing everyone who had been ready for some drama and excitement in their dull lives. We later found out that Olga had been missing her parents.

To Alpona's displeasure, Olga spent a lot of time with Ajoy's grandmother. She felt threatened by their companionship. They were obviously conspiring against her. One evening, Olga surprised the family by cooking the most wonderful fish curry, potatoes with poppy seeds and sweet mango chutney — all the Bengali dishes that Ajoy loved. She served the food to everyone, speaking in a little Bangla with the cutest accent. The family was impressed and showered her with compliments. Alpona looked sceptical and enquired casually about her newly-acquired cooking skills. Olga announced that it was Granny who had been grooming her.

The ailing Granny was looking healthier now. She proudly announced how Olga had ensured that she takes her medicines on time, even the bitter ones. 'Yes Bouma,' granny nodded to Alpona. 'I ken also talk eenglis now!'

The family burst out laughing as Alpona almost fell off her chair. She smiled as she realised that the firangi bride had conquered all differences and won the hearts of everybody in the family, including hers.

Nandita Chakraborty Banerjji

The Resounding 'Yes'

My father had arranged a meeting to 'see' a boy for the umpteenth time. Somehow, all his earlier efforts had come to naught, thanks to my less than perfect looks. I had 'seen' a man with saucer shaped ears, who thought he was God's gift to womankind. Boy, was I glad he decided I was not worthy of that gift!

Then there was this really dark complexioned guy with bloodshot eyes. But guess what, he didn't want to get married to me because I was too dark. I thanked God for this guy's audacity.

Another guy came from Hyderabad to Mumbai. Must say his honesty would put Satyawadi Harishchandra to shame. He told me in the midst of our 'meeting' that he was to see another girl in Pune the next day. Had he liked me, he would have not gone but now he would have to make that trip. He assured me, though, that if the girl was worse than me, then he would come back and we could get formally engaged in a couple of days. I was supposed to feel honoured, but mercifully, the Pune girl was not worse than me.

The very first boy I 'saw' was my cousin's best friend. I was all of nineteen and had gone to spend the vacation at my cousin's. No sooner had I entered the room than he, Atul I think his name was, took me aside and embarked on a monologue about how he was still struggling and we would have only our love to survive on, if he decided to marry me, that is. Naïve that I was, I directly told him I wasn't interested in him. That was the end of my 'freedom to voice opinion' in a democracy. He put the whammy on me because that day on, I was destined to be rejected by suitors, however unsuitable they were in my opinion. I almost started enjoying the discomfort of these poor guys and the innovative ideas they came up with to say 'no' to marrying me. But in the bargain, I got a pair of hyper tense parents who became frustrated and lost hope of ever finding a son-in-law for themselves. I had stopped protesting and would quietly go whenever any meeting was set up just to keep my parents happy.

This time was different, I did not want to go. I had just taken my exams and I was going with my friends to Matheran. I had earned this holiday and seeing a boy squirm wasn't fun enough to give up a weekend with friends.

My mom was at her tragedy queen best and it was easier to succumb to her wishes than to suffer her melodramatic behaviour. So the next day, I went to the pre-determined hotel room and as a sign of revolt, I did not put on any make-up. Not that putting on make-up ever helped, but still. As soon as I entered, I heard barely disguised gasps. I was used to all this by now. It was like a record playing over and over. I could see their disapproval and the boy's mother looking visibly let down.

When the boy decided that his answer was 'yes', the family looked shocked as if a death sentence had been pronounced. His sister rushed towards him, barely masking the fact that she wanted to convince him to change his mind. I looked at myself in the mirror on the opposite wall and wondered if there was something demonic about me, maybe triple digits branded on my head invisible to me! I was also perturbed that in case I did get married to this particular boy, his family would probably hate me and make my life miserable, also hold it against me for taking their son away.

Through the entire hullabaloo, I noticed the mother looking intently at her son. She paid no attention to the rest of the people trying frantically to make the boy see some sense. She came quietly towards me, held my gaze for a few seconds, and what she did next floored me. She removed her gold chain, showed me how the ancient-looking pendant held deep meaning. It had been in the family since eons and every subsequent daughter-in-law had worn it as a sign of acceptance, as a sign that she had been welcomed into the family and she would be protected and cared for in times to come.

I was shaking visibly. While I knew my fate was sealed, I marvelled at this woman who had decided to have faith in her son's choice and take a chance on me, knowing that she would be facing the wrath of her family and community members. This wise-looking woman set my mind to rest as she welcomed me into the family and gave me her blessings. She is the one person who singularly made everyone change their mind and the one to whom I owe a lot for making me one of the happiest brides, not to mention my parents for being the most relieved people on the planet.

And later, when I found out the truth about my husband, I had more to be grateful for... He had clearly indicated that he was not vegetable shopping and had accepted me even before seeing me.

Shashi Agarwal

Welcome Lady Wife

Army brat to Army wife: the metamorphosis seemed an exciting one, and being a lady wife (had anyone heard of a gentleman wife ever!) saw me in a different avatar altogether. My brand new husband was posted in Bhuj, in the Rann of Kutch, a place which came into prominence only after the killer earthquake slammed it onto the map years later.

As we neared the station, my husband said half jocularly, 'Be prepared to transform yourself into something resembling a bride. There will be a reception committee to receive the new bride at the station, and tea at the Mess thereafter!' To say my knees were already quaking at the prospect was no understatement!

Luckily there was no fire on, and the lady who came to receive us at the station said with a smile that lit up her face, 'Come, we'll get you home. There you can change into a nice sari perhaps!' Her glance at my jeans and T-shirt was quizzical. Not exactly what an Army wife was supposed to wear! Luckily that viewpoint has made a discreet exit these days.

Home turned out to be a cute little flat, which my husband

had thoughtfully done up with mustard curtains, a refrigerator from which I gulped down a glass of ice cold water, and a Sumeet mixie which was to last us for the next decade. Then was makeover time, as I hurriedly donned a pink silk sari, hunting around for matching earrings, and completing the look with a dab of lipstick and kajal.

The Officers' Mess soon loomed before us. My heart was beating frantically as my husband gave me a quick smile, which did not help in the least as I had no idea what lay before me. My gaze fell on the tall fair lady who stood at the entrance with an aarti thali in her hands. This was the Commanding Officer's wife, the first lady, who was waiting to perform the customary ceremony to welcome the new bride. As we stood in front of her, she passed the lit lamp thrice around before us, applied red vermillion on our foreheads and smiled, saying, 'Welcome to the family!'

A number of faces filled my vision, all waiting expectantly, and I felt like an exhibit in a glass case. However, all the gazes were filled with genuine warmth, and the banter that followed indicated just how popular my young husband was, as gory tales of his exploits as a bachelor caused much merriment and made me feel quite at home.

Over a cup of hot sweet tea (the first of many I was to have over the years!), wafer thin sandwiches, mini samosas and biscuits, I was gently enveloped by the bonhomie and warmth of that family which would be mine for over twenty years or more.

At the end of the tea session, the Commanding Officer welcomed me into 27 AD Regiment and then it was time to leave. As the crowd followed us outside, broad smiles on their faces, I noticed a huge vehicle outside. The next moment there was a shout, 'Heave, Gopi!' and I found myself picked up by my husband and hoisted onto the back of the vehicle. Luckily, I was pint sized and as I settled myself down, I sensed some movement inside. As my eyes got accustomed to the darkness after the bright sunshine, I noticed the Regimental band waiting patiently for us.

The mystery was solved soon enough. A senior officer motioned to all the bachelors to get in alongside with us with the stern injunction, 'Make sure that the vehicle does not move beyond ten kms per hour!' A bottle of rum had been promised to the band, which suddenly responded enthusiastically and began playing for all they were worth. I was red with embarrassment and so was my better half, who promised them two bottles of rum if they piped down. But, of course, that was not to be, as they smiled, watching their sa'ab turning red in the face.

And so we crawled on, traversing along all the tiny bylanes and the wider avenues of Bhuj town, as the band got louder and louder, and the townsfolk came out of their houses to gawk at the brand new bride. When we finally got home, I was exhausted, but the overwhelming welcome and the friendliness remained with me even as I dropped off to sleep.

Years later, the whole rigmarole was repeated, as a brand new couple stepped shyly over the threshold of the Officers' Mess, but this time I was at the other end — the Commanding Officer's wife performing the customary aarti to welcome another new bride into the fold. As I passed the aarti thrice over around them, my thoughts winged back to that first day, when I had first set foot in this most amazing Regiment, and become a part and parcel of it. So much water has flowed under the bridge since then, and my love and regard for our Regiment has only grown stronger over the years.

Deepti Menon

White White Face

My friend Maria had always wanted to marry an Indian man. She was fully Caucasian, but during our college days, was bowled over by bhangra performances and Bollywood music. Also, there were all the clichés about Indian men in America, all becoming doctors or lawyers. At least once a week she would tell me, 'Sue, I want to marry an Indian guy. Our kids can break in to bhangra whenever they are happy.' I would laugh it off.

Last month, Maria married Arvind, an Indian man who she met at medical school in the United States. Even after three years of dating, she had no idea about Indian families. Arvind's parents had moved to America when they were in their thirties. The weekend after his proposal, she saw Indianness in its full bloom.

The newly engaged couple flew to India to meet Arvind's relatives. Maria was used to living with her mother since her second birthday when her parents got divorced. In India, she came face to face with heat, humidity and twenty people at the door of her fiancé's family home in suburban Mumbai.

She was wearing a saree and folded her hands to greet everybody as Arvind's mother had advised her to. After five first cousins and some aunts and uncles took her suitcase upstairs to the guestroom, a wrinkled old lady came forward and took a long look at Maria. It was a critical look. My friend was shocked at the outright stare and was sure she would not like the lady. Two minutes later, this family member was introduced as the grandmother.

She could not speak English and gestured to Maria to sit in front of her on a very low divan covered with bolsters. My friend tried her best to sit down straight-backed in her sari. Arvind was meanwhile dragged away by cousins who were seeing him after two years.

The barely five-foot-tall lady asked Maria to sing. She looked flustered as the aunts and uncles encouraged her to sing. Maria managed to drone out a few lines of the last Hindi song she had heard on the plane, 'white white face' from the movie *Tashaan*. The old lady looked at her in shock while the aunts clapped and laughed merrily. Then Maria was asked to dance. She felt like a clown being asked to perform. 'I can't dance. I really can't. Mujhe maaf kijiye,' she said in broken, American-accented Hindi. The old lady started grumbling in Hindi, leaving Maria close to tears.

Maria did not interact with the grandmother for the next four days of her visit. She only saw her looking at her constantly and felt uncomfortable.

Next month, the wedding took place in California. The first ceremony was held at a church to honour Maria's mother's faith. Then there was a Hindu ceremony at the local temple.

Arvind's grandmother and one aunt and uncle made the long journey to the States. Maria did not notice much around her during the ceremony, she was having trouble managing the heavy veil and jewellery. While the bride and groom were walking around the fire seven times, somebody caught her eye. The old lady was smiling at her from one corner of the room, two teeth missing from the top row, but eyes lit up. Maria had thought that she hated her so she did not know how to respond. Plus, she was trying hard to understand the steps in the rituals.

That night, after the Hindu wedding, there was a party at a hotel. A DJ and dance floor stood next to a buffet of Indian cuisine. Maria was glad to be able to wear her gown after the afternoon's heavy finery. She joined Arvind for their first dance as a couple. After the song ended, they were leaving the dance floor. 'STOP,' yelled out a thin but strong voice. The whole party turned to see the grandmother standing next to the DJ. She put up a frail hand and said, 'Now dance.' The DJ played the 'white white face' song from *Tashaan*! Maria realised that the old lady actually liked her. She went up to her and gave her a big hug.

Sue Ghosh

11

TIMELESS WISDOM

No man is truly married until he understands every word his wife is NOT saying.

−Author Unknown

A Mother's Wisdom

A trip home before the wedding is awaited with fondness for any bride-to-be. It is usually a trip filled with emotions for the parents and their daughter. I had planned my visit home four months before my wedding for the Gowri pooja. I was looking forward to all the attention and pampering. However, my trip home was very high on emotions as things took a drastic turn.

A day before I landed, Appa had a heart attack. Amma kept the news from me till three hours before I boarded the flight. I don't think I reacted to the news. I just didn't know how to react and I think by the time I had digested the news, there was so much else to do that there was no time to react.

This was the first time in the last fifteen years that Appa was not at the airport to receive me. Amma was there with friends but Appa's absence really tugged at my heart. On our way home, I chatted with Amma and asked her how this had happened. It was a very normal conversation; no one was emotional. We were both just dealing with the situation. We got home, rested and then after a couple of concerned phone calls from friends who had heard about Appa, Amma and I left for the hospital.

Appa was in the ICU when I first met him. He looked happy. He was definitely enjoying all the attention everyone was showering him with but this had certainly rattled him. Amma was her usual calm self; more focussed on what to do and how to do it.

The first week of my vacation was largely spent at the hospital. Once Appa came home, things were better. It was the first time I had spent so much time with him as he was advised complete rest: no office, no evening walks and no socialising.

While Appa was under complete rest, Amma was fulfilling her duties by being a 'Super Mom'. Along with managing the home, Appa's health and diet, Amma was single-handedly driving me around town from malls to tailors to the spa. I knew she was tired but she wanted to ensure that I got most of my shopping done and that at the end of it I had a good holiday.

The Gowri pooja was the highlight of the holiday. Amma managed to organise a get-together in two days. It was important as it was the last pooja before my wedding. We invited many of our friends home. I did try and discourage Amma from having a big gathering, but she wouldn't hear of it.

The last two nights of my vacation we went to my favourite restaurants for dinner. My holidays home are never complete without trips to these restaurants. Poor Appa sat most of the evening without eating at all, quite a tough task for a foodie like him.

Saying goodbye was the hardest. I just didn't want to leave them this time. It was the first time in many years that I cried at the airport ... something I didn't do even when I was twelve. I guess that was the first time I reacted.

Getting married, for reasons I don't know, is always an emotional phase for a girl. I knew that my life in the months before my wedding would change and I'd be going through so many feelings and emotions. So yes, in a way, I was prepared for the emotional ride. But when you see the first man in your life down, there is something scary and unsettling about it. And then you see your mother being strong for you and him, ensuring that you have the best vacation, you understand the complexities of the many roles you will have to play.

Without the use of many words, Amma had shown me who I would have to be in the future. A supportive mother, a responsible daughter and most important, a wife whose strength helps her husband be strong. The wisdom I gained from Amma's actions is something I will treasure forever.

Vibha Karnik

An Ode to the Perfect Bride

A chance allotment of rooms in the hostel made me her neighbour. I will call her S. She was a year senior to me. Before we realised, we became good friends and loved sharing a cup of tea from the hostel mess in the morning. And both of us also enjoyed soaking in the mild Delhi mid afternoon winter sun while preparing for our end of term exams. S was a brilliant student and she was chosen for a prestigious scholarship to pursue her PhD in the United Kingdom.

Before leaving for the UK for three years, she decided to tie the knot with the guy she had been dating for four years. And as they decided on the marriage date, we were all excited to have our share of fun and enjoyment. As they had opted for a registered marriage, they had to put up the notice a month in advance. In that one month, I experienced something that changed a lot of things for me in the years to come. Both of them had parents who lived in West Bengal and Tamil Nadu respectively. There were no sleepless nights over the wedding preparations. There was no need for calculations, negotiations and counter-negotiations to manage the expenditure. For me, it was like watching a film from a new genre. I had grown up in a society where marriage meant the girl's parents losing their sleep over making never ending gift lists for the bride-groom's ever-expanding family that included innumerable chachis, buas, mamis and masis. And the weeks prior to the marriage always involved making endless trips to jewellers' shop sari shops and the like. I had always seen harried members of the family running to the market for some last minute shopping.

S's wedding preparations were as fresh as the autumn evening breeze. This was one wedding which revelled in the mantra 'Less is more'. For the wedding cards, they chose lovely handmade paper from Delhi's Khadi Bhandar. A friend who had mastered the art of calligraphy did wonders and beautiful wedding cards were given as invites.

Just two days before the wedding, their parents came and stayed at the university guest house. After registering the marriage, we all returned to the guest house. As S's father chanted Sanskrit sholkas in his deep voice as part of the Hindu ritual to bless the newlyweds, many of us couldn't control our tears. It was a moment of great joy and happiness, not only for the young couple, but for all of us who had seen their love grow.

The next day saw a reception party organised by them. The venue was the community hall of the university. There were no orchids flown from Holland, no fireworks or even red carpets. A sense of camaraderie and elegance ruled the evening. Dressed in a South silk sari (without any visible make up), S glowed like a queen. And her husband was looking handsome in a traditional Indian outfit (what a welcome break from his regular jeans and kurta). As a perfect tribute to their mixed marriage, the guests were treated to steaming idlis, hot vadas and other Southern delicacies and the dessert was rosogollas. Holding each other's hands, they mingled with the guests and received best wishes and hugs with a smile. As talented friends strummed guitars and sang songs with gay abandon, the air smelt of love, joy and pure bliss. In that moment of happiness, I could not help but see S's parents sitting on the chairs and enjoying the songs and the celebratory mood. Till then, I had never seen a bride's parents enjoying their daughter's wedding so much, without a trace of worry that something might just go wrong.

A few days after the wedding, S took a British Airways flight to London to pursue her higher studies. And a few years later, I also got married on a November morning, sans extravaganza. As a true senior, S had showed me the way. I just had to follow her. Now years later, when I look back, I feel a sense of pride. For S, the perfect bride.

Deepika

Father of the Bride

I was sure that Sangita's parents would never approve of me dating their lovely daughter, but I continued nevertheless.

I had just acquired a management degree and was looking for a job. My father gave me a measly pocket money of two hundred rupees every month which had to be spent sparingly, so I planned the cheapest dates possible.

The first time, I asked Sangita to meet me at a bus stop. As luck would have it, it started raining heavily. By the time she arrived, I was drenched and looked like a crow that had just hopped out of a puddle. The date ended in five minutes.

The next time we decided to meet, Sangita told her father that she was invited for lunch to her friend Usha's place. I waited behind a truck parked outside her house to whisk her away like a valiant knight as soon as she stepped out. Within a few minutes, Sangita was escorted out by her father and they got into a taxi. She popped her head out of the window and winked at me as the cab sped away. I boarded a bus and travelled five kilometres to Usha's house. Sangita laughed at my cowardice.

After a few days, I took her to a small restaurant. As soon as the food arrived, Sangita muffled a scream. It was not the dosa; it was her father with three of his colleagues who had seated themselves on a table next to ours. She nudged me to hide in the restroom. I panicked and rushed into the ladies' toilet. There was a little uproar, and when I came out after fifteen minutes, our table was empty. Sangita had taken flight.

It was getting increasingly difficult to simply hang around in public places, so we decided to go on walking dates. On one such outing at the park, we bumped into her neighbours. They looked at me suspiciously. Before Sangita could say anything, I introduced myself as a distant cousin of hers from the US. They commented on our resemblance and walked away.

Sangita was furious and refused to meet me on the sly. It had been a while since we had met. I was anxious and decided to visit her house with an excuse of returning a book. I rang the bell and her father opened the door. He asked me if I was a salesman but I mustered up courage and asked for Sangita.

I was let in, only to see the same neighbours whom we had met at the park, sitting in the living room. I contemplated slinking away like a scared hyena but they were too engrossed in a discussion to notice me.

Taking a deep breath, I tried to initiate a conversation with her father, but he looked at me sternly and asked if I was the boy who hid in the toilet in a restaurant, got drenched in the rain, took his daughter out for long walks and was her remote cousin from the US!

I was stunned. I stammered and tried to explain myself. He glared at me for a few moments and then burst out laughing.

He informed me that Sangita had been brave enough to tell him everything. Her honesty had won him over and he even told me that once I settled down with a good job, he would talk to my parents for our marriage. I was overjoyed and at the same time, ashamed of myself.

That day I learnt a great lesson of life from Sangita who believed that courage and truthfulness made life simpler and saved one a lot of embarrassment.

Contrary to the expectations of a lot of people, I achieved a lot of success in my life. I owe it all to my wonderful bride who transformed my attitude and thoughts. It is because of her that we stand together, hand in hand, weathering the storms of life and sharing our happy moments cheerfully.

Debashish Majumdar

Indifference — Abuse of A Different Kind

I was like any other ordinary Indian girl. Demure, shy and reserved, you could aptly call me the girl next door. You would find me holding my grandmom's hand and helping her to the nearest seat. Or you would find me at the cardiologist, with a white plastic bag in my hand that contained my grandparents' medical records. Every old lady would invariably try to shower me with obvious blessings, such as 'may you find a good groom' or 'may your life be filled to the brim with joy'. Not a day went by when my name would not be heard resonating a million times through the hallway of my home.

I had a lot of dreams about my wedding. Not the rich, hi-fi lifestyle, although money is an important factor; but my dreams were of emotional fulfilment, companionship and a lifetime of togetherness that I had seen my parents share with each other. Our community is a small close-knit one, with most of the families sending their '12th pass or B Com' sons abroad in search of work. Higher education is a rare attribute among people in my community.

One cold day in November, seventeen days before I turned twenty-six, I got married. It was a match made in heaven. He was five foot eleven inches, fair and handsome, with an American accent to boot. Most people exclaimed, 'Perfect pair!' What could go wrong?

Second day after marriage, he went into a fit of anger that lasted throughout the night. I was dazed. I couldn't understand. But he had issues with his parents that I came to know about in due course of time. This continued regularly. He had yet to find a job. That added to the whole mountain of worries. He blamed his parents for forcing him into the marriage. His bouts of anger convinced me that he had a heart of stone. At my birth home, I had never ever heard the expletives he used against his parents. We fought a lot about this, with me defending his parents. In two months, he had ended all ties with me. He maintained a sweet detached rapport that would muster no questions. He had a knack of saying all the right things so that people would just shut up and stop bugging him.

I held on, hiding everything from my in-laws, in the hope that he'd change once he found a job. I convinced myself that he loves me, but is depressed. I decided to overlook the fact that he was neglecting me completely. No one in the world knew what was happening (rather, not happening) behind closed doors. I had gradually become invisible to him, reduced to being a showpiece in a corner of the bed, tearful, neglected, sick and depressed. Six months passed and I was feeling suicidal. Then I started to speak out to him and protest his behaviour. I wanted to know why I was the one being punished for no fault of mine. 'How long will this go on? Life has come to a standstill from the day we got married. I have feelings. I need love too.

Please,' I begged and implored him to change. I thought he'd understand, but he termed it as 'nagging' later on.

He finally found a low-paying job abroad and went away, with promises of getting me there so that we both could work and start life anew. I never knew what was in his mind when he waved goodbye at the airport. He never called me. I realised that he had cut his brother and sister off from his life too. No reasons given. Just like that. And he had done the same with his parents earlier. He was doing it to me now.

That was the last straw. I knew I had to take a stand. It was now or never. A voice inside me said, 'Once a door mat, always a door mat.' I blurted out the entire ordeal to my parents and in-laws. My parents were shocked. His parents assured mine that they'd take stern steps and make everything alright. Three months passed — they weren't trying hard enough. They acted complacent. I wasn't informed of any of their conversations; maybe because they had nothing to say. He refused to talk it out. He had gone underground. He had escaped to a new life, never to return.

I started getting panic attacks. I lay on the bed, with vague memories of my mom-in-law rubbing my hands and trying to call my relatives. In an hour or so, the panic attack had subsided. But I declared that I could take no more. I was going back. I called my parents up and asked them to take me away.

After coming back, I had a lot to think about. What I had conjured up as love was actually disgust in his eyes. Disgust I refused to see because I was so in love with my husband. He did not speak to me for five months. Yet, he did not miss me. I had given my all to the marriage; to the extent that I was pulling on single-handedly. He just left me. He deleted me from his memory and his life. I had to accept a lot of facts later on. The biggest being that he had never accepted me. He used me to get back at his parents. He soiled me and left me alone. He didn't think I deserved an explanation.

My mistake was that I kept suffering silently. I hid everything even from my parents because I wanted to save my marriage. He took advantage of that and happily let me think about so much of the 'love' he had for me. But his deception was an eye-opener for me.

I am turning twenty-eight now. I have a lot to do. I have to complete my Masters and find a job. I have to be the son my parents never had. There are too many responsibilities. Too much time was lost.

And, I learnt: Love yourself enough to protect your own rights. You deserve every joy in life. Don't depend on a man so much that you lose your sanity while he coolly doesn't care. If he can't love you back, he is not worth your love. Give yourself a chance. Give yourself a beautiful life. You have wings. Fly.

Punam J. R.

Letter to My Sister

It was a manic Monday as my to-do list spilled onto the second page: List of possible playschools for son's admission, leave approval from boss for visiting in-laws, renewal of the insurance policy... The responsibilities were endless. Visions of my carefree days long gone by flooded my mind but were soon taken over by apprehensions about the countless roles that came with marriage.

I brooded and sympathised with myself when suddenly my phone beeped. It was a text from my sister Aparna who had got married a couple of months ago.

'Hi, I just had to tell you how much the "letter to my sister" is helping me. On many occasions I have found it to be so relevant and true. It has been a precious gift! Thank you!'

I didn't remember the contents, so I searched through the sent items of my emails to read the letter I had once written to my sister.

Dear Aparna,

As your wedding day draws closer, I can't help but feel nostalgic. The black sheep of the family is getting married. My memories of you go back to us playing as kids. It was amusing how you used to love watching advertisements, and hated losing even one mark in exams. And here you are, at the threshold of a new life with Ninad. I wish you all the best for everything.

I want to give you some tips as an elder sister. Some of them I have learnt from Ma, some on my own. Keep the ones which are useful; trash the ones which are not.

So here goes...

Family is important. Your parents, his parents, siblings, everyone. You need to keep them all together. You are the common link!!!

Sometimes, people make comments casually. They will hurt you. If they are Ninad's relatives, talk to him about it. Chances are they never meant to say it the way you perceived it. Remember he knows his parents and relatives better than you do. So trust him when he says they didn't mean it and then get it out of your system.

In the first few years, you will need to go out of your way to love your new family. Small gestures and words of appreciation go a long way. Believe me, it's worth the effort. You will see them reciprocate much more.

Never ever let anyone challenge your self respect. If faced with such a situation, maintain your dignity and make your point firmly (not rudely).

Spend lots of time with his mother! She will tell you stuff about Ninad which you will always cherish!

Always treat his parents well. No matter what, they have raised him to be the man he is. They deserve to be treated with respect and love. Try and remember this when you feel they may be unreasonable.

Remember that your perspectives may not always match. Agree to disagree. This is valid for your husband and his parents too!

Lastly, always be yourself. Just as you need to accept your new family as they are, they need to accept you as you are.

As you enter this beautiful world of love and marriage, let go of all your inhibitions.

It's a rollercoaster ride and well worth it!

Always here for you.

Love,

Aditi

Another beep reminded me of my son's vaccination and got me out of my reverie. But I was smiling and found myself reliving the wonderful journey I had embarked on four years ago. It was indeed a rollercoaster ride with occasional lows, but innumerable highs. Suddenly my to-do list seemed shorter, and the obstacles seemed to evaporate. With renewed vigour, I finished the day's tasks, and went back home early to play with my son.

As I lay down that night, I typed a text which would surprise my sister.

'Thank you! For reminding me that this roller coaster ride of marriage is worth every high and low!'

To this day, whenever my morale needs a boost, I always read this letter, and stay inspired forever.

Aditi Patil

Morning Tea

She was entering a new household. New to her in more ways than one. It was an inter-community marriage, and she was new to the customs of the family she was joining. She was a Bengali and he was a Kumaoni.

Moreover, her husband, the youngest son of the house, was not the best of sons. He had rebelled all too often in matters of education, career, and now, marriage. She lived in a world of books and romance. She was given to poetry, imaginative flights, dreams and the like. Not exactly the ingredients to make a very good daughter-in-law.

With trepidation, she stepped out of her room that first morning and went into the kitchen. Her mother-in-law was up and about already. She gave her a plate of biscuits and two cups of steaming tea to take to her room.

She took them to her husband.

'How many cups have you brought? Sit down here beside me.'

'No, I can't, I have to see about the work in the kitchen.'

'Then take one cup back into the kitchen,' he said gruffly.

She took it back.

'Why have you brought it back, beta?' her mother-in-law asked. 'I had given them for both of you.'

'But, what about lunch?'

'It can wait. Come after some time.'

'Oh!' she said and smiled.

'Go on,' her mother-in-law was insistent. 'You should sit and have tea with your husband in the mornings. This is the only time you'll have in the years to come for having an uninterrupted talk with him. When you have children, you will see that they will need your constant attention later in the day. And your husband will also go away to work. This is the time when you should sit with him and plan out the programme for the day and discuss all important engagements.'

How true her mother-in-law had been. How could she, a woman so removed from the pressures of modern-day living, have known this? For years, the morning-tea ritual was treasured and adhered to by her. Years passed... Her daughters were born, grew up and went away to college. Yet, the morning routine remained the same. The first cup of tea to be had with her husband.

Even when she had started working, this was one part of her life that did not change. In those moments of tranquillity, as she sat preparing for her lecture to be delivered at the school in which she taught, while her husband read the morning newspaper, they found an understanding that began the day on a positive note.

All matters of discord, spoken or otherwise, all petty squabbles of the previous day were dunked in the cup of morning tea. Over the cup of hot chai, visits to the doctor's clinic for their childrens' inoculations were planned, parent-teacher meetings were prioritised and later, problems of growing children were discussed. Money matters, health issues, social commitments and heady dreams — all topics found a place at that time. For that was their own private time. Maybe, on some days, not a single word was exchanged, but the silence which cocooned them in the mornings was a warmth which glowed in their hearts throughout the day.

Her own mother had not included this when she had advised her about so many things before marriage. It was her initiation as a young bride and the words spoken by her mother-in-law on that first morning that she had to thank.

Monika Pant

Rethinking Tradition

Ekta's parents were ecstatic. Dipesh was a great guy. They were happy that their daughter had found someone like him to spend the rest of her life with. The families celebrated the engagement with great joy and were soon plunged into the thick of wedding planning. While the venue, guest list and decorations were all important, Ekta's father had something more significant on his mind — the actual wedding.

One evening, he called Ekta for a little talk. 'I spoke to the panditji today and have booked his dates for the wedding, but I think we need to discuss some important details about the ceremony.'

'Sure,' replied Ekta, putting aside the colour swatches she was holding.

'You have attended many weddings and seen how the groom is welcomed with great joy and grandeur. We have several rituals that we perform without being aware of its significance. But I think that we should look at it more deeply. I am not sure how you feel, but I do not want to do the kanyadaan.' Ekta was taken aback.

'Before you say anything, let me explain,' he added seeing the confusion on Ekta's face.

'If you analyse the word itself — kanyadaan — it means giving away of the bride. It indicates that the bride's family is separating themselves from her. But I don't agree with that. I don't think that we are giving you away with this marriage. I feel that I am gaining a son.'

Ekta was moved by her father's sentiments. Her parents had always been firm believers in social justice and gender equality, and this suggestion was a reflection of that.

They were lucky to find a pandit who was willing to understand their emotions and co-operate.

The wedding ceremony began. At the moment of kanyadaan, the pandit paused and conveyed the bride's father's perspective to the groom and his family. There was an awkward silence for a couple of minutes. Dipesh looked at his father-in-law and said, 'Thank you, Dad!' There were murmurs and sighs of relief.

Everybody gave approving smiles as Ekta's father welcomed his son into his family.

Heena Patel

To Me...

If I could go back in time
To my wedding day,
For the young bride that was,
I'd have some things to say.

Forget about the relatives,
At least the ones who don't matter.
They're just there for the free goods,
Loads of gossip and idle chatter.

Ask for whatever you want,
It is your special day.
You have the right to jive and hoopla,
To do the funky chicken and shout 'Hooray!'

Keep your best friends by your side,
Don't let them out of your sight.
They'll mop your sweating brow,
And get your make-up looking right.

Spend ten minutes with your grandparents,
Let them bless you with all their heart.
Their words of prayer and blessings,
Will keep your sanity from crumbling apart.

Give your brother a giant hug;
Maybe tweak his nose for good measure.
Tell your parents that you love them;
That being their daughter is a blessing and a pleasure.

Concentrate on the rituals,
You wanted a traditional wedding.
There's beauty and there's reason
To what the priest's saying.

But most important, darling girl,
Remember now and always –
It doesn't matter, the last two kilos;
It doesn't matter, the three strands of greys.

It doesn't matter you're not five inches taller;
No, it doesn't matter you're a little short.
It doesn't matter, the boys who were mean.
It doesn't matter you're not the sexy, stick-insect sort.

You are truly a beautiful bride today,
As stunning as can be;
You're getting married to the man you love,
And in your eyes that's plain to see.

It is this love and happiness,
That joyous sparkle in your eyes,
That make this day so worth it,
You lovely, blushing bride.

Baisali Chatterjee-Dutt

12

TREASURED MOMENTS

Our wedding was many years ago. The celebration continues to this day.

—Gene Perret

A Bride's Dilemma

Seven steps around the fire, the chanting of mantras
The showering of petals, the exchange of garlands
The red vermillion on my head
All tell me that I'm entering a new phase of my life.
The person who sits by my side, holding my hand in his
Is practically a stranger to me, I've known him only a few
months.
Is that enough to determine that we can live together for a
lifetime?
I look at the crackling fire; I listen to the mantras
All around me there are shouts of jubilation
The ceremony is complete and we are now man and wife...
My father puts our heads together, to bless us as one
I cast a furtive glance at my new husband
He turns to look at me, his face breaking into a smile
The grip on my hand tightens
Vowing to bind us for life
That moment is one I'll treasure forever
For therein lay the promise

That through thick or thin; through a loss or a win
Through joy or tears in all the coming years
We were bound together.

Divya Bhatia

Adieu

I had thought that I would spend the last week just talking to her, pampering her, giving in to every whim and fancy of hers, sharing the last moments before she passed into a different phase of her life. I thought I would spend every waking moment talking, talking, just talking, as though to squeeze out the very last drop of togetherness with her before she got married. God knows where the days went. Time flew by in a whirlwind of fittings, sending out invitations and endless list-making. I still had those words unsaid when the D-Day arrived. Even the last night before the wedding I spent in last-minute preparations in a frenetic pace; and did not hug her tightly enough.

Suddenly, in the midst of a house full of guests, I found myself alone with my daughters. Well, almost. The beautician was putting the last minute touches to the bride's make-up. My elder daughter. I paused to look at the radiance emanating from her face. Resplendent in red and gold, she looked wide-eyed at me and asked, 'Am I looking alright?'

What could I say? To me, she was always the most beautiful girl on heaven and earth. My angel, my cherub. I nodded, not trusting my voice. My younger daughter also seemed more mature all of a sudden, probably realising for the first time that her idol, her friend for all seasons and supporter in all matters was no longer going to be around and she would have to fend for herself. I gazed at them. My daughters. The bride and the bridesmaid. I wanted to stop the moment and tell the guests to wait. I wanted to tell her to sit down and spend some time with me. But there was no time.

We had to leave for the venue. I watched as she was surrounded by her chattering and laughing cousins and friends, who escorted her into the car waiting at the gate of our house. I stood for a moment in the now-empty house, a kaleidoscope of images whizzing past my eye. A little girl in a red uniform, whose hand I held tightly as she went out of the gate to board the school bus… A teenaged girl who turned and waved at me at the gate, when she went for a movie with her friends… A college student who carried her own luggage when she walked out of the gate as she left for another city. Today, she was going out of the gate as a bride and when she returned she would be a married woman. I firmly closed the latch as I left.

The strains of the shehnai mingled with the hushed whispers of the guests, when she entered and was escorted to the stage for the *jaimaal*. I watched mesmerised with eyes misted and a smile on my lips. My Thumbelina had grown into a fairytale princess. Later, when my husband took her hand and gave it unto our son-in-law, I saw the same misty-eyed look on my husband's face. In the poignancy of the moment, the mixing of unrestricted joy with a tinge of sadness gave an unreal quality to the night.

That night I understood the complex dichotomy of life. The mellow happiness mixed with a pang or two of apprehension. The heavy footsteps of a bride's parents are contrasted with the spring in the step of the bride and the bridegroom. That day I understood the feelings of my own parents when I had got married. From one generation to another, the very same emotions are passed. The circle is completed and the balance is maintained.

Monika Pant

Bride-in-Waiting

My engagement was sudden, and the marriage too soon for me to get to know my fiancé well. We were in different cities and did talk on the phone but I soon realised that Subhash was a man of very few words. His remoteness made me uncomfortable and I would ponder over it for hours, turning myself into a nervous wreck. Finally, I decided to wait and watch what the Almighty had in store for me.

Two days before the wedding, I flew down to Ahmedabad. I had a greatly romanticised idea of marriage, which is why, despite Subhash's lack of enthusiasm, I was very eager. It was my wedding after all.

To my alarm, there were over fifty people at the airport to receive me! My heart skipped a few beats as I waded through the waves of near, and very distant cousins who looked overly happy to see me. My eyes explored, between the hugs, handshakes and a lot of feet-touching, but my beloved was nowhere to be seen. Any apprehensions creeping up were pushed down by the weight of the fifty garlands around my neck.

Two days of wedding celebrations and innumerable rituals in the sultry month of July passed in a haze without taking me any closer to the mystery man I was now married to. I was convinced that Indian weddings were deliberately designed to ensure that one gets no time for wedding jitters or a second thought. The experience was like an avalanche and the sudden calm after that was unnerving, as one wonders what was worse.

We were soon off to Langkawi for our honeymoon. Finally, when it was just the two of us, Subhash fell asleep even before the flight took off. My company wasn't good enough for him to want to stay awake! I wondered if he realised that his distant behaviour drew me closer to him. As I looked at him closely for the first time, his stern face and sharp features made me turn to jelly and I felt a tug every time he glanced at me. It was definitely the Mills and Boons effect. His expressions, on the other hand, were unreadable and his dark eyes gave away nothing.

The island was beautiful. The honeymoon destination was my idea as Subhash would have probably chosen to take me to Frankfurt, where he goes for work frequently. I would have been the bride-in-waiting and he would be at some office, negotiating deals. That was certainly his idea of romance.

We got into our swimsuits and settled down under a gazebo at the beach. There were people zipping around on the water scooter, skiing and playing volleyball. I asked Subhash hesitantly to take me on the scooter. As expected, he refused and I wondered if this man sitting next to me had any feelings for me at all. I went back to longingly watching the excitement around me.

There was a young man riding the water scooter as his two daughters took turns sitting with him. He ensured the thrills by taking sharp turns and making the ride a bumpy one. As they got out of the water, it was impossible not to notice the guy's stunning good looks with his blue eyes and blonde hair.

'Hey, was it scary?' I asked him on an impulse.

'Not at all. You should not miss this!' he replied breathlessly.

'Will you take me?' I asked again, surprised at myself.

'Anytime. Let me drop the kids to the hotel and I'll be back.'

No sooner had he left that–Subhash looked at me and said, 'Come on, I'll take you, why did you ask him?' Was that a hint of jealousy that I had detected? I was elated. Needless to say, I had a fantastic ride and I am sure he did too because when he did let his guard down for a few seconds, I actually saw him smiling.

Later in the evening when we got into the pool, I noticed Subhash swim to my side when the blonde-haired guy entered the pool and waved to me. He held my hand under the water as if staking his claim. It felt wonderful and even though he never said it in so many words, I knew what he felt. I knew I would no longer be the bride-in-waiting.

Shashi Agarwal

Bride's Day Out

The atmosphere was palpable with excitement. There was a flurry of activity all around me. Everyone seemed to have something to do. I was the only one left out. I looked at my hands and feet, all adorned with mehendi from the previous night. The havan was at 4 p.m. followed by the chuda ceremony.

My mother looked as though she would burst into tears any moment. Dad, who was usually unruffled, was also looking a trifle nervous, an expression that was so alien to his personality. My younger brother, who I had never seen working, was bustling around looking extremely busy. And to top it all, even my college friends, who had travelled from Baroda to 'be with me' decided to gallivant around Delhi and shop at Janpath (twenty-five years ago, there were no malls and I still believe that the pleasure of shopping on the streets is unparalleled).

Where was I in all this confusion? The poor neglected bride-to-be? And here I thought I would be the centre of attention. I was excited, nervous and scared all at the same time, and there was no one I could share my feelings with.

My grandmother sat with the packers, supervising the wrapping of the gifts that needed to be given, while my grandfather was regaling my young cousins with one of his famous anecdotes.

The shrill ringing of the phone suddenly pulled me out of my reverie. It was probably a relative calling to wish us luck. My grandmother, who was usually reluctant to pick up the phone, did so when she saw that there was no one else to take on the task.

'It's for you,' she said .

I picked up the phone to hear my fiancé's bright voice on the other end, 'Hi, how're you coping?'

'Ok I guess,' I said, close to tears.

'Hey what's up? With just a day left, I thought you'd be counting the minutes!'

'I know, but everyone seems to have something to do, except for me. I feel lost and terribly unsure.'

'Guess what?' he chuckled, 'I feel pretty much the same! What say, I pick you up and we go out for a bit?'

'Today?' I nearly choked at the thought, 'just not possible! Who'll let me?'

'You don't have to ask — just slip out — with everyone so busy, no one will even notice.'

'I'm not so sure.'

'I'll come around in fifteen minutes and wait downstairs.' (This was way before the advent of mobiles).

'Fine, I'll try my best.'

I could feel Biji's ears perk up. For a person who did not know English and generally claimed to be hard of hearing, she was suddenly alert.

I had to tell someone and though normally Biji would not be my first choice, she was partly in the picture already.

'Kya hua?' she asked, 'you want to go out?'

'May I?'

'Well,' she said hesitantly, 'it's not the right thing, but better than have you moping around. Come back soon.'

'I'll be back before you even know,' I promised.

I was true to my word and returned within the hour, feeling happier and more at ease.

My co-conspirator was pacing up and down waiting for me. She carried our little secret to the grave.

The first my parents will learn of this is when they read this story…

Divya Bhatia

Charlatan Bride

I just found this story about the exploits of an unusual charlatan bride so cute that I had to share it with my friends. It's about my friend Rachita and how she was a year-long bride. Puzzled? Let me start at the beginning. I met Rachita and Parimal a few months ago and was awed by the radiant glow on Rachita's face. When I got to know that they had been married more than a year ago, I couldn't resist the urge to ask her how she managed to retain the proverbial 'bridal blush'. She smiled and with a twinkle in her eye told me this story much to the chagrin of her husband.

Rachita and Parimal were extremely fond of travelling to exotic locations but before they got married, they hardly had any time, both being busy studying, and later with their careers. Their honeymoon was short too as they had already taken leave much before the wedding, as Indian weddings are known to have elaborately long drawn out festivities for days together.

Soon after that, they went on their first real holiday. Whilst checking in, the manager asked, 'Honeymooners?' and Rachita, avoiding the eye of her mortified husband, replied unabashedly with the right amount of coyness thrown in for good measure, 'Yes!' The delighted manager immediately upgraded them to the honeymoon suite.

In the evening, when they returned after dinner, there was a tiny cake, just enough for two, nightcaps with a candle lit, and last but not the least, a bouquet of red roses, laid out on the coffee table. Rachita says, 'It made me feel so special, and I cherish all these little moments that made me remember my honeymoon.'

The next vacation was Venice and Rachita told the receptionist that they were on their honeymoon. 'Rach!' Parimal exclaimed, disgruntled at her behaviour, but Rachita was unapologetic and said, 'So what! It's a long honeymoon.' This time though, Parimal was wowed by the treatment they got. In the evening, they ditched the vaporetto for a gondola ride on the Grand Canal. Suddenly, the gondolier broke into a romantic serenade. When the enraptured couple offered a tip, he refused saying it was a gift for the newly-wed couple from the hotel they were staying in. It had been a fairy tale holiday for both of them as they were transported back to the not too long ago wedding night.

Once, Rachita says they stayed in Edinburgh in a smallish bed and breakfast place, there the woman caretaker would bake muffins and scones for them every evening and when she changed the sheets every evening, she would wink at them shyly, which made them go red in the cheeks.

Parimal, who by now was feeling left out, recounted the

time when they went to Devigarh in Rajasthan, the beguiled manager went overboard with his extravagance. Early evening, he had called in their room to ask what time they would like to have dinner. At the appointed time, an escort came to pick them up, but instead of taking them to the restaurant, he led them through a narrow staircase winding itself in curves dipping down, and sometimes going up, which opened up onto a small terrace with jharokhas on either side. There was a small mattress laid out with a low table in front of it laden with a veritable feast, not forgetting the bucket of ice with champagne in it. That was not all: An old turbaned man played the jal tarang, producing the most maudlin of melodies.

Feeling all mushy and romantic, when they entered their suite, they were stupefied at the sight that greeted their eyes. White satin gowns and satin slippers were laid down on and below the bed. Candles lit everywhere, wedding shlokas being played on the CD player and the huge lotus shaped marble bath-tub filled to the brim with rose petals floating on top. 'Rachita had worn a red coloured salwar kameez that day and she reminded me of the way she looked on our wedding night,' says Parimal.

Once they had even got found out when another friend of theirs checked into the same hotel and blurted out the truth. They had been embarrassed no end when the vexed manager almost threw them out.

All this had been a lark but Rachita says more than the fun they had, the feeling of being a bride time and time again had been of paramount importance. The love they had and their passion kindled kept them mesmerised, which was what was extraordinary.

So now I knew the secret of the beatific after-glow, and I cannot help but feel envious mingled with regret at not having a chance to experience the same.

Shashi Agarwal

Judgement Day

My mother stayed hungry that one big day of the year —
Karva Chauth. My father is a non-believer who has always
been against the idea of fasting. But when it came to THE fast,
he was extremely supportive, not for any self-serving interests,
but just as an indulgence. So once a year, Dad would be up
when mom sat at the table to eat her sargi early in the morning.
The large mug of tea that was to last her through the day was
always brewed by him.

When I got married, I started my mental preparation for
Karva Chauth, until the big day arrived.

I decided to use this as an opportunity to judge my husband.
The poor man had no idea of what was going on in the mind
of his wicked to-be-hungry-for-the-first-time two-month-old
wife.

Conscientious as he is, he set his alarm, after consultation
with my mother, and woke up at the first 't-r-i-n-g', so that I
wouldn't get disturbed. He then switched on the geyser and
waited for the water to heat up. After that he tried to wake

me up. It was a cold November morning of Ambala. I 'oohed' and 'aahed' and went deeper into my quilt. After a couple of attempts, he said, 'Okay, forget the fast and go back to sleep.' I jumped out of bed.

Since we were staying in a mess accommodation, I did not have a kitchen. To eat my sargi, we had to drive five kilometres on a bike, to a friend's house at 4.30 a.m. By the time we reached, we were frozen. My husband watched me as I ate. I tried to ignore the indulgent smile on his face. How can one possibly eat paranthas, nuts, fruits and everything else at 5 a.m.? I didn't miss any opportunity during the day to remind him of this and the awful effect it had on my digestive system. I succeeded in generating a deep feeling of guilt in him and he even offered to not eat his lunch. 'How will that help?' I frowned.

The day passed by slowly. In the evening, once again we left for our friend's house for the pooja, on the bike, with me in my bridal finery, holding the thaali and everything else I was supposed to. I waited impatiently as my husband went out in search of the elusive MOON. He managed to spot it through the trees and the clouds. I had lost my appetite and felt too exhausted to even try and fake joy, to keep up the mood and spirit of the occasion.

It was now time for that one sip and one morsel I had been craving for, earlier in the day. After I had 'seen' the moon, my husband asked me to close my eyes, and open my mouth. I waited and wondered what all the shuffling sound was all about. Just then, lovingly and clumsily, he shoved a large slice of Chandigarh-imported chocolate cake into my mouth,

greasing my face with the icing! For a moment I was surprise
and then we laughed till I had tears in my eyes. I looked at
my husband tenderly. The poor darling was unaware of the
fact that it had been judgment day for him... And that he had
passed with flying colours!

Minnoo Singh

Kichhu Hobey Na

To the disappointment of my brand-new husband, I refused to ride on the old, family scooter. My in-laws had never come across someone who had a phobia of riding on two-wheelers. 'Kichhu hobey na (nothing will happen),' they reassured me, each time I described in graphic detail how I would fall from the skidding scooter, crack my skull and land up in a hospital for a month.

It all began in my college years. To politely refuse unwanted bike rides, I would simply say, 'I'm scared.' How was I to know that this harmless declaration would get wired in my brain? And who could have predicted my marriage to a man who loved his wheezing, swaying scooter more than the two smug cars sleeping soundly in the garage?

The clash continued. Situations that required the services of a scooter cropped up mysteriously. Whether I had to be picked up from the local railway station in a jiffy, or we had to visit the market, each time my husband's eyes lovingly picked out the scooter. He believed it was 'so very convenient'. I refused to budge. He went ahead on the sputtering thing while I walked.

I pointed out the hazards of using a two-wheeler, narrated the data of scooter accidents in gory detail and talked of the vulnerability of the rider. He responded with facts on accidents involving cars. I insisted on the instability of the vehicle which he countered with praises of its manoeuvrability. When I told him I preferred the comforts of a car, he chided me for being selfish and not thinking of petroleum conservation. I cursed the terrible machine that was creating a rift between two sensible and otherwise perfectly happy human beings.

To top it all, the scooter took on the airs of temperamental opera singer. On some days, a gear malfunctioned and at other times, the brakes acted strangely. On cold days, it showed its contempt for carrying mortals by refusing to start. My husband kept up his efforts, with it and with me.

And then one day, I got trapped into a ride by my dear husband. I congratulated myself for having recently made out a Life Insurance Policy and mentally ticked off all the lovely things I had done on planet earth. Saying my last prayers, I sank with a sigh upon the back seat, my eyes staring blankly at the swirling world around me (I discovered later that it was my dizziness!).

And then... Exhilaration! The wind rushing through my hair, the sunlight dancing in crazy patterns on trees, the determined growl of the engine, the grey road rushing forward and blurring past; it felt wonderfully free! I called myself a fool for having deprived myself of such pleasures for all these days. Out of sheer politeness, my husband refused to comment as I plunged headlong into the world of scooter rides.

Strangely, I found myself getting late for work in the morning and my husband would offer to drop me off at the station, to save me a long walk. Needless to say, I grabbed each opportunity. My in-laws watched with open-mouthed puzzlement. Their chicken-hearted *bou* now enjoyed zooming rides with reckless glee.

Today, each time my husband and I step out of home for a merry trip on the cool machine, Ma gently tells her son, 'Shabdhane chalash (Drive carefully).' To which I turn around with a grin and say, 'Kichhu hobey na!'

Piya Mukherjee

Making the First Move

As I was the eldest of three sisters, my parents were getting worried about my marriage. I was in the last year of college but they already thought I was over the hill and went around with a worried expression on their face.

Though I was widely popular with both sexes in college and had many guys propositioning me (and raving about my beauty), I was a total failure in the arranged marriage scenario. I went through all the exercises of boy-coming-to-see-me without a demur, but somehow not one said 'yes'!

I always wondered at the dichotomy of life. Was it my dusky complexion which my friends actually found beautiful, but cut no ice with a typical Indian male.

Finally someone said 'yes' to me.

Fourteen people from my husband's side had come to 'see' me. They looked at me with x-ray eyes, hoping to find as much fault as they could with my nose, skin, hair, clothes, etc.

But my to-be-husband said 'yes' to me and whispered softly in my ears that if I liked someone already (or did not like him) I could tell him so and he would take the onus and say 'no' to me. This was the time when if the boy said 'yes', the girl's affirmation was taken as granted.

I looked at my to-be-husband with new found respect. In my family, where men are aggressive with bad tempers and never seem to see a woman's point of view, this man was like manna from heaven.

I just whispered a 'yes'.

My parents were ecstatic. Finally I was getting married and now they could concentrate on my younger sister.

I met my fiancée a couple of times before our wedding. He was soft spoken and we could not go beyond holding hands.

Is it me, I would wonder. Why doesn't he hug me? Has he said 'yes' because of some failed love affair? My mind would be running wild with the most improbable stories where I was the unwanted bride.

We got married on a wonderful rainy day.

Our suhaag raat room was beautifully decorated. We went in. I went in to have a shower, came out in a modest night gown. My husband went in to change and came out in a kurta pajyma.

I switched on the AC. I could only see one thin bed cover. 'You use it,' he said, 'I don't feel so cold.' And then he added, 'You must be tired, let's go off to sleep.'

Tired and sleepy on my wedding night, I stared at his words.

No way was I going to let this happen to me.

I looked at him and then I just hugged him hard and said I have been wanting to do this for a long time.

He reciprocated by holding me tight too and that was the beginning of an ecstatic night and many tempestuous nights to follow forever and ever.

Sometimes, brides have to make the first move. Bridegrooms may be willing, but can be shy too!

As told to Anu Chopra

Moments in Time

I had a modest nikah ceremony at home. Nomi, my twenty-year-old sister, battling leukaemia for the past year-and-a-half, suddenly lost all movement in her legs that afternoon and had to be hospitalised immediately. She died thirty-five days later, hanging in there until I returned from our short honeymoon in Singapore. But this is not a story about the tragedy; it is about the wonderful time I spent with my sister before my wedding.

Trousseau shopping is that one time in your life when you can indulge yourself without any guilt and even have people encouraging you to buy more. Nomi accompanied me to Hyderabad, though she was tired and recuperating from her bone marrow transplant. But we would set off every morning to the lanes of the old city of Hyderabad that tempts you with bales of shiny, glittery fabric and sparkling bangles. Nomi picked up a beautiful traditional Hyderababi khada dupatta to wear for my reception, but never did.

We also took an unplanned trip to Madras. It was great to see the wild, heaving sea as we stopped by the Marina Beach and spent a quiet afternoon there. I held a sunshade over Nomi for most of the time as the sun was beating down fiercely. I didn't feel tired and my arms didn't ache. I was just so happy to be with her when she was well, and not locked up in a dark hospital room, reeking of pain and fear. I felt I could hold that sunshade forever!

Back home, the wedding preparations were in full swing. My sisters and friends had decided to put up a dance performance for the mehendi. Nomi and I spent many happy hours writing down the names of songs we wanted the DJ to play, and ran to several music shops to get them recorded. We also choreographed the dances ourselves and Nomi came up with some typical Bollywood moves. We had so much fun those evenings, with a dholak and a tape recorder, fooling around and laughing at each other's awkward steps.

Sadly, Nomi was in too much pain to dance at my mehendi. She had developed a severe pain in her back a day before the functions began. We later found out that the cancer had resurfaced. There was not much hope now and Nomi had refused further treatment. Her immense courage and patience had helped her withstand the severe chemotherapy and the painful bone marrow transplant. But now she could not take it anymore.

The wedding was over and Nomi left us soon after for a better world, where she could finally rest in peace.

For a long time after she was gone, we kept all her possessions in her cupboard, just as she had left it. She was meticulously neat and her cupboard always looked like it had just been arranged... It even smelt of her. After a few months, we decided to give her stuff away to charity. We found many new things Nomi had never worn, and learnt a bitter sweet lesson: To live more in the moment and enjoy our small pleasures and possessions. Use your new clothes, wear your new shoes. Life is short.

We found a beautiful note pasted inside her cupboard that read: 'My spirit can never be taken from me, for it is the part of me that is eternal.'

We used it in her obituary. She had obviously prepared herself for what was to come, and had made her peace with destiny.

It was almost as if Nomi had waited for my wedding and honeymoon to get over before drifting off into a deep sleep, leaving me deprived of the most special friend one could ever have. Today, God has blessed me with my own spirited little girl, much like my beloved sister, who refreshes great memories of the days I spent with her.

Zainab N.S.

The Unknown

Other than his name, I knew nothing about him. Even that I overheard, no one told me what it was. Indeed, throughout my wedding ceremony, it was as if I didn't exist, like someone else was going through the experience.

Our priest had told my parents that his family was looking for a 'match'. He was described as 'skinny, very intelligent, no temper (what a lie!), well-dressed, okay-looking and wheat-complexioned'. I was witness when my mother repeated this to a neighbour. No one told me anything, leave alone ask. My father didn't believe in talking to the family, but I didn't find that unusual for none of the fathers I knew talked to their children in those days. It was the norm. I wanted to know, though, and the more they hid from me, the more fiercely curious I became.

It was my marriage that was being discussed in whispers: 'The boy is in the Air Force.'

'He lives in Assam, but the quarters and the salary is good.'

'He comes home for Deepavali every year.'

'No vices? Yes, he drinks liquor, it seems, but nowadays these boys...'

'A wife like Tara will do him good. Our Tara will make sure he won't drink.'

'They want a wife who will follow traditions.'

'Our Tara knows all the pujas, shlokas, rituals. They will have no problem.'

'She's been looking after the house since she was a teenager.'

I hung around, eavesdropping as much as I could. For the ceremony, I guessed, I would have to wear a nice sari, lots of ornaments, as I'd seen my cousins do. Classmates used to giggle about the first night, I smiled with them, ignorant and innocent of what it meant.

The engagement was a brief, fleeting event where I didn't get a chance to even register his features. I was busy serving, flitting in and out of the kitchen, helping Amma with the chores, clearing the table, answering silly questions: 'How much sugar would you use if you had to make payasam for ten people?' 'How much washing powder would you need if you had to wash three saris?' The general talk was about booking the hall, visiting the ancestral village on so-and-so convenient date, checking out the auspicious muhurtam, deciding upon the caterer (menus were fixed), booking tickets for the journeys, etc. No one really cared whether the groom or bride felt or thought anything at all. I threw a glance at my 'to-be', found him staring at me and I fled from the room in embarrassment. I was literally pushed back into the room when 'those people' were to leave... And I had to touch everyone's toes.

He had to do the same to my family elders and that was when our eyes first met and held intimate, unshared moments of togetherness. Naturally, my pilot memories of him are of, and from, silly angles.

The weeks that followed were hectic. Tailors and jewellers had to be visited. Banks, too. No idea where so many relatives turned up from, the house was so crowded, the bathrooms forever occupied, the kitchen full of smoke and smells and me... I was bombarded with tons of advice: 'Make sure you look after your mother-in-law well.'

'Behave like a cow for five years, then reign like a queen.'

'Don't even think of wearing those new-fangled clothes. They will think we haven't brought you up properly.'

'Brown is a decent colour. All your blouses should be brown, grey or black. They go with everything and you are not so fair that you can wear pink or green.'

Indeed, my gorgeous silks with brocade borders were worn with white petticoats with frills at the bottom and those hideous, ill-fitting blouses.

When I grumbled about how mismatched they were, one aunt teased: 'Who's going to see them? It'll be so dark.'

Muffled laughter.

'What-what-what?' I asked, a bit boldly. I was getting pampered with oil baths and flowers and yummy food and attention. It had done wonders to my confidence, for sure. 'What-what-what?' I asked again.

My mother shushed me up and said something I have remembered for many nights, something long decades away, I can still recall with crystal clarity: 'No matter what he does to you, don't scream.' Everyone looked away, some seriously, some shyly, some stifling laughter. But no one contested that advice, nor added to it.

Those words had shaken me up considerably. Conditioning demanded that I don't question anything.

Through the ceremonies, the sticky, humid activities, the hunger, the tiredness... Through all the stroking of my head by elders and holding of hands by my cousins, I had just one thought jogging through my mind: Whatever he did to me, I wasn't to scream.

The first few nights, there were too many relatives for us to be together. Indeed, I didn't even know we were supposed to be together. So naïve was I. Sigh. Finally, the excitement settled down and we were given a room to share. The fact that I'd have to change in front of him unsettled me terribly. I was too shy to say anything to my mother-in-law or even my sisters-in-law, so I decided not to change into another sari. Those were pre-nighty times. He didn't bother, just took off his trousers and shirt (horrification! I didn't know where to look) and wore his pyjamas. Then he looked quizzically at me, indicated that I should sleep next to him and waited for me. I took a l-o-o-n-g time, and crept onto the mattress only when he was asleep and I was drop-dead tired.

It was a couple of days later that we touched. Held hands. Came closer. Every morning, the rest of the family gave us strange looks. I hadn't screamed. I hadn't had any reason to. It was many days before he did that something and when he did, I didn't want to scream.

As told to Sheela Jaywant

Twisted Ankle

Rhea had twisted her ankle! Well, it was no big deal except that she was in the midst of her pheras!

After dating for four years, Rhea and Vicky were finally getting married. There was resistance from both families but they had dug their heels into the ground. They tried all possible means to convince their parents, but nothing worked. They threatened to elope. The parents relented. They could certainly do without a scandal.

The wedding would take place after three months. Considering the degree of the confrontation they had faced, the couple expected frosty treatment from both sides, for a while. But, they were in for a surprise. Rhea's parents welcomed Vicky into the family with open arms. He was pampered to the hilt at every visit. Vicky's parents showered Rhea with all the attention deserving of a to-be daughter-in-law! Everybody seemed to have taken a complete u-turn!

Rhea was a die-hard romantic. The furore of resistance (which she thought was rather thrilling) had subsided, and she looked forward to a 'perfect' wedding. It sure seemed to be happening that way. The families were not just happy, but very enthusiastic; the wedding preparations were on in full swing and she was on top of the world!

It was the wedding day. Adorned with white orchids and pink lilies, the mandap looked like a part of heaven. Vicky looked dashing in a white sherwani and a gorgeous Rhea tried hard to keep her eyes off him. The pandits chanted the mantras in chorus, creating a magical ambiance. It was all perfect!

After the rituals, it was time for the pheras. For the first six pheras, Rhea would walk behind her groom, and for the seventh phera, Vicky would walk behind his bride. This signified that both man and wife should be willing to follow the other if required, in any situation of their life.

It was all so idealistic and Rhea looked dreamy-eyed as she moved forward for the last phera. That is when she stepped on her heavy lehenga and twisted her ankle. The pain was sharp and she could barely stand! The parents were alarmed... It was inauspicious and the phera had to be completed! Rhea panicked... She didn't want to look stupid, limping around the sacred fire with the help of a dozen eager aunts. How could she be so clumsy and spoil it all? She was terribly embarrassed and hurting as tears rolled down her cheeks.

Just then Vicky whispered something into the pandit's ears. The pandit deliberated for a few seconds and then gave a nod of approval. Vicky gave a reassuring look to Rhea's parents and then whispered into her ears, 'Hold on tight, Baby!' Before she knew it, he had lifted her in his arms! Rhea was stunned for a moment. She then looked lovingly into his eyes as Vicky completed the phera, amidst murmurs of 'how romantic'; 'isn't that sweet' and 'what lovely photographs this would make'!

Rhea was delighted! She had the most romantic moment a bride could ever have... Thanks to her twisted ankle!

Swati Rajgharia

More Chicken Soup?

Share your heart with the rest of the world. If you have a story, poem or article (your own or someone else's) that you feel belongs in a future volume of Chicken Soup for the Indian Soul, please email us at cs.indiansoul@westland-tata.com or send it to:

Westland Ltd
S-35A, 3rd Floor
Green Park Main Market
New Delhi 110 016

We will make sure that you and the author are credited for the contribution. Thank you!

Contributors

Abhay Chawla is a trained electronics engineer from IIT-BHU. He switched professions and is now into journalism and social development. He currently teaches at Delhi University and lives in Gurgaon. He can be reached at gurgaonharyana2008@gmail.com.

Aditi Patil works for an MNC bank, and loves wielding the pen in her spare time. She writes at sunshine-in-a-box.blogspot.com. She is a life coach, specialising in helping people achieve their life goals through affirmation and other techniques, and also conducts workshops at MBA institutes. She can be reached at patil.aditi@gmail.com.

Amrita Srinivasan is a part time writer, part time painter, part time marketing professional and a full time mother of two. Her cynicism and satire is borrowed from daily life. She can be reached at c_amrita@yahoo.com.

Anu Chopra is an Ahemdabad-based writer. She has published a book of short stories called *Scattered Thoughts*. She loves reading, especially women-centric Indian fiction. She can be reached at anuchopra77@gmail.com.

Archana Mohan is a business journalist from Bangalore. She is a sports fanatic and a murder mystery addict. She blames global warming for her disastrous culinary skills and thanks God for instant noodles. She blogs at archanamohan.wordpress.com.

Travelling, writing, reading, partying, practicing and conducting training in alternate therapies in her spare time and just gazing and enjoying nature's bounty makes her life worth living. **Aparna Shankar** works in an MNC to earn her living. She can be reached at scriba.soul@gmail.com.

Arti Sonthalia is a young, budding writer, from Hyderabad. Her work is dedicated to the lotus feet of her Guru, whose presence has brought colour to her life. She can be reached at 13artiag@gmail.com.

Aarti K. Pathak is a professor of Economics, freelance writer and a travel enthusiast. Her literary works have been published in several leading books and magazines. She can be reached at aartikpat@gmail.com.

Abha Iyengar is an internationally published writer, poet and scriptwriter. She writes on travel, health and spirituality and conducts creative writing workshops. Her collection of poems *Yearnings* has been recently published. She is the recipient of the Lavanya Sankaran Writing Fellowship for 2009-10. She can be reached at abhaiyengar@gmail.com.

Abhilasha Agarwal works with a society called Kritagya that looks after the old and the aged. She writes poetry and fiction, and has been published in the *Statesman* and the *Times of India*. She is the author of the e-book *Vibrant Palette*. She can be reached at abcal37@yahoo.co.in.

Avantika Debnath, also known as Avni, believes every pleasant story should be shared with the world. However, some stories that do not have a pleasant end should be given a pleasant turn and left incomplete. She can be reached atavantika.debnath@gmail.com.

Baisali Chatterjee Dutt is coming to terms with the fact that her boys have up-an-growed on her. As she reaches mid-life crisis, she is making out a bucket list which she plans on laminating if not exactly following. She also writes and has just finished compiling *Chicken Soup for the Indian Friend's Soul* and is working on the next title.

Debashish Majumdar is a marketing professional. A popular award-winning author, poet and playwright, over a hundred of his short fiction works have been published, broadcast and one made into an animation film. He can be reached at debcreations@rediffmail.com.

Deepika wakes up every morning dreaming of starting a cafe in the mountains. But then reality hits her hard and she rushes to earn a living. She's passionate about life, words, music, biryani, Darjeeling tea and the Indian Railways. She can be reached at mencuckoo@gmail.com.

Deepti Menon has been a writer for as long as she can remember, and loves the sheer thrill of seeing her name in print. In 2002, her book on life as seen through the eyes of an Army wife — *Arms and the Woman* — was published. She continues to write for various magazines and publications. She can be contacted at deepsmenon_7@yahoo.com.

Dhanya Venugopal is a software engineer from Kerala who currently resides in Dubai. Apart from blogging, she is also passionate about Internet Marketing and is always trying out new methods to kick-start her online business. She can be reached at electroscribbles.blogspot.com or dhans.v@gmail.com.

Divya Bhatia is a postgraduate in Nutrition from MSU, Vadodara. She has been in the field of education for over 20 years. Married to an Army officer, currently she is heading a leading school in Chandigarh. An avid reader, her articles concerning education appear frequently in local newspapers. She can be reached at divibee@hotmail.com and divya.divibee@gmail.com.

Divya Nair Hinge is an avid reader and a writer who has been published in several leading publications. Born and brought up in Mumbai, her marriage to a Naval Officer gives her an opportunity to travel far and wide. She's currently working as a Public Relations Manager for a reputed MNC. She can be reached at divyarkn@rediffmail.com.

Fatima M. Noronha's non-fiction work has featured in national and regional publications in India, as well as online. The BBC broadcast one of her short stories, while others have appeared in periodicals and anthologies in India and overseas. She works as a mum, gardener and freelance editor. She can be emailed at fmn2011@gmail.com.

Ghazala S. Hossain has been writing ever since she cares to remember. Her short stories and poems have appeared in various publications. She lives in Kolkata with her interior designer husband and two school going children. To read her blogs, log on to ghazala.sulekha.com/blog/posts.htm. Write to her at msghazalahossain@gmail.com.

Heena Patel is an environmental engineer-turned-classical musician from Canada, currently living in India. She is a tabla player under the tutelage of Pandit Divyang Vakil and is working for the preservation and promotion of Indian classical music. She blogs at rhythmicthoughts. wordpress.com and can be reached at heena.tabla@gmail.com.

Hema Dhawan is a writer based in Bangalore. She enjoys writing short stories and poems. In her leisure hours, she likes to read and meet new people. She can be reached at hemadhawan08@gmail.com.

For **Laisram Indira**, people are a way of making memories along life's journey. She can be reached at ilaisram@gmail.com.

Irene Dhar Malik edits films, television shows and documentaries. She also writes print and online features as well as for film and television. She has written short stories and novellas for online sites. She loves traveling and is a mother to her in-a-hurry-to-grow-up daughter.

By day, **Jamshed V. Rajan** (also known as Jammy), is Director - Products, India, at Nimbuzz and by night he is a wannabe stand-up comedian. He blogs about his wife and life (and in recent times, his three-year-old daughter too!) at ouchmytoe.com. He can be reached at jammy@ ouchmytoe.com & 09971996581.

Born in Edinburgh in 1944, **Jane Bhandari** has lived in India for 39 years. She is the author of two collections of poetry: *Single Bed* and *Aquarius*. Her poems have appeared in several anthologies, most recently in Sahitya Akademi's collection of Indian women authors, and in literary magazines. She also reviews poetry.

Joie Bose Chatterjee has worked as a free-lance journalist with the *Telegraph* and is a regular contributor to the *Statesman*. A social worker, she was earlier involved in teaching English and Dramatics. She is currently working on her first collection of short stories and can be reached at joiebose@gmail.com.

Kiran Manral is a Mumbai–based freelance writer. She blogs at thirtysixandcounting.wordpress.com and karmickids.blogspot.com. She can be reached at kiranmanral@gmail.com.

Komal G. Kudva is currently working at a finance organisation. She loves to spend time with her daughter. In her free time, Komal indulges in reading, listening to music, writing poems and surfing the net. She can be reached at komal573@gmail.com.

Lona is a doctor in Bangalore.

Mariya Salim is working in Bangkok as an editor of a magazine that promotes interfaith dialogue and peace. Writing fiction, reality or otherwise, is her favourite thing to do. She can be reached at mariya. salim@gmail.com.

Meena Murugappan is a sixteen-year-old pharmacy student from Fairleigh Dickinson University, New Jersey. She was born in India, raised in Zambia and now lives in the United States. She is an accomplished Bharathanatyam dancer, a passionate writer and an avid reader. She can be reached at meenamrina@yahoo.com.

Minnoo Singh has been married to an Army Officer for twenty-eight years. Transfers and travel, and her work as an educationist, have enriched her personality and widened her perspective. She has been associated with various aspects of writing and is presently a freelancer.

Mira Pawar is a freelance writer who has written feature stories for *Gulf News*, Dubai. She has also freelanced for Khaleej Times, Dubai and is now based in Hyderabad, India and freelances for Speakbindas.com; Suite101. com and Triond.com. She can be reached at mirapawar@gmail.com.

Mita Banerjee has enjoyed almost four decades of working as an educationist and writer. As a writer, she has written extensively on subjects ranging from the environment to issues related to women and children. In 2002, she was awarded Woman Achievers Award for journalism. She can be contacted at mitabaner@gmail.com.

Monika Pant is a mother and an English teacher. She stays in Lucknow and is a regular contributor to the Chicken Soup for the Soul series. She is currently writing three novels. She can be contacted at mpant65@gmail. com.

Ever since **Monisha Sen** accepted that being a mother day and night was boring and not good for the kids, she went back to working. As she couldn't handle her demanding job, she now works from home as a trend analyst (for money) and a writer (for fun). She can be contacted at sen. monisha@gmail.com.

Mudra Rawal, working as a software engineer, is based in Pune. She strongly believes that everything and everyone around her has a story to be unearthed. You can drop her a word at mudra.rawal@gmail.com.

N. Chokkan (Naga Subramanian Chokkanathan) is a software consultant by profession, and author by interest. He writes in his mother tongue (Tamil) and English and has authored many books. He blogs regularly at nagachokkanathan.wordpress.com and can be reached at nchokkan@gmail.com.

Nandita Chakraborty Banerjji is a creative writer and her first novel is in the process of being published. She also writes short stories. She can be reached at nandita.banerjee@gmail.com and nandittabanerjee@gmail.com and +91-9819320762.

Neelima Varma is a teacher by profession but has decided to be a full time home maker. Having a degree in Child Psychology has helped her in her teaching career as well as with her own kids. Reading is in her blood. She can be reached at neemavarma@yahoo.com.

Pallavi Shankar is a beauty writer with *Marie Claire*.

Parul Gupta is a Delhi-based freelance writer/ editor / research analyst. An Economics postgraduate from Delhi School of Economics, she reports/contributes occasional features to *Sunday Deccan Herald* and stories to the Chicken Soup for the Soul series. She can be reached at parulmudita@hotmail.com.

Piya Mukherjee is a merchant banker-turned corporate trainer and professor. While she enjoys her extensive travels for work, Piya 'recharges' herself by pecking away at her laptop. She can be reached at piyamukherjee7@gmail.com.

Prerna Uppal is a London-based freelance writer who loves to do anything that has to do with words, be it reading, writing or playing around with them. A postgraduate in communication studies, she has reported for *Week*, the *Indian Express* and CNN-IBN. She can be reached at prerna.uppal@gmail.com.

Priyanka Kadam has written short stories, essays and poems that have been published in magazines, anthologies and on the internet. She takes time out to promote the welfare of orphaned children of HEAL, a charity taking care of 1000 orphans. She can be reached at priyanka.kadam99@gmail.com.

Punam J.R. is a freelance SEO copywriter and content writer. She has successfully executed various content writing/repackaging projects for a global clientele on behalf of Chillibreeze Solutions Pvt Ltd., and Hop Higher SEO Dubai. She blogs at punamlr.blogspot.com.

Based in the US since the last eleven years, **Pushpa Ramachandran** has been juggling with a career in software, freelancing with local Indian magazines, blogging to find her true call, managing the home front and has a teenage son to add to the fun and medley of life.

Raamesh Gowri Raghavan is a poet and writer by night, and a copywriter by day. He lives in Thane near Mumbai and is considered funny company by his friends (at times). He can be reached at azhvan@yahoo.co.in.

Rajika Malhotra is a voracious reader. Hailing from Mumbai, she is now based in Ahmedabad. She can be reached at rajika22@hotmail.com.

Rana Siddiqui Zaman is a journalist and works with the *Hindu*. She is the co-author of a book on media that is a part of the syllabus for media students at Heidelberg University, Germany. She can be reached at ranaafrozsiddiqui@gmail.com.

Ranjini Sharma is a software engineer. Formerly from Bengaluru, India, she has been living in USA for twenty years. Her hobbies are graphics design, painting, pencil sketching, gardening, furniture designing and much more. She can be reached at RanjiniSharma@gmail.com.

Ranjani Rengarajan-Deoras works in the media and reads for passion. Her sole aim is to write a good book one day and is waiting for inspiration to hit! She can be reached at ranju17@gmail.com.

Rehana Ali is a school teacher, an aspiring writer, loves adventure tourism and has travelled widely. She hopes to compile all her stories and essays into a book of short stories which will bear the title 'Short Stories for all Ages'. She can be reached at ali.rehana@gmail.com.

Revathi Seshadri lives in Nagpur. As a person of leisure and a keen observer of life, she has an eye for the ridiculous and loves to present incidents in a humorous vein with no malice intended. Her email id is revathi.seshadri@gmail.com.

Richa Wahi is a Kolkata-based teacher and teaches language skills and creative writing. She also works as a training consultant with the British Council, conducting workshops for young learners. Richa enjoys travelling and cooking. She can be reached at wahiricha@gmail.com.

Ritu Goyal Harish is a freelance journalist and writer who believes in activism through the press. She writes exclusively for the *DNA* (*Daily News & Analysis*) published from Pune and is known for civic/ investigative exposes. She can be reached at ritugoyalharish@gmail.com.

Roohi Bhatnagar is a wannabe writer. She also develops software for a living, apart from following her dream of being a published writer. She has contributed to other titles in the Chicken Soup for Indian Soul series. She welcomes everyone in her virtual world at roohibhatnagar.com. She can be reached at roohi.bhatnagar@gmail.com .

S. Meera is a work-from-home-mother of two. Though writing is her profession, she is eagerly awaiting her first published novel. She has also written, compiled and edited coffee table books. She can be reached at meerasampath@hotmail.com.

Shanaya Mody is a post-graduate from the London School of Economics and Political Science. She is now running her own business in Ahmedabad, India. She is very excited to be marrying Arunabh Khatua in December 2010! She can be reached at Shanaya_m@hotmail.com.

Shashi Agarwal is a home maker and a mother of two daughters. She likes a bit of reading and writing. She can be reached at agarwalsash@ gmail.com.

Sheela Jaywant is an author/writer/translator based in Mumbai. Her books include *Quilted* (stories of middle class India), *Melting Moments* and *Liftman and Other Stories*. She works in the administration department of Hinduja Hospital and can be reached at sheelajaywant@yahoo.co.in.

Shifa Maitra is a media professional who lives and works in Mumbai. Writing is her passion and she is a creative director at UTV Bindass. She can be contacted at shifamaitra@gmail.com.

Smita Pranav Kothari is pursuing her Masters in Journalism at Harvard University. She loves writing about relationships, concocting creative ideas and vegetarian international recipes, travelling and watching romantic comedies. She can be reached at smitapkothari@gmail.com

Sreelekha Chatterjee is a researcher and an editor and is also a trained singer. She considers creative writing to be her true passion. She can be reached at chatterjeesreelekha@gmail.com.

Sue Ghosh is a Kolkata-based journalist. She can be reached at sud24@hotmail.com.

Sutirtha Saha, a computer engineer in an MNC, lives in Hyderabad with his wife and two sons. His hobby is writing short stories/poems and he has won Shankar's International and other awards for his writing. He can be reached at sutirtha.saha@gmail.com (blog:sutistories.blogspot.com).

Swati Rajgarhia is currently working as a professional editor. She is an eager writer and loves to read. She can be reached at swatirajgarhia@yahoo.com.

Teja Lele Desai, a journalist, lives in Mumbai with her soulmate. She loves the mountains and the sea, reading all that she can lay her hands on, movies, good food, Maggi and Harry Potter. She's also big on DIY projects, collecting recipes and travelling. She can be reached at tejalele@gmail.com.

Vandana Vij can be reached at vijvandana@rediffmail.com.

Vaishali Shroff is a part time business development consultant, full time writer and an over time mother. She loves to read and write short stories. She can be reached at vaishali.shroff@gmail.com.

Vaishnavi Verma is a software engineer and a Communications graduate. Books, chess, food and travel are the keywords among her many interests. She is an enthusiastic blogger and a short story writer. She is currently based in Mumbai and can be reached at vaishnavi.ankush@gmail.com.

Veerendra Mishra is a police officer from Madhya Pradesh. He is fond of writing fiction, short stories, articles on social issues and the like.

Vibha Karnik is a Bangalore-based marketing communications professional. A dreamer, a planner, an optimist and a complete idealist, Vibha enjoys watching and reviewing movies and travelling. She can be reached at vibhakarnik@yahoo.com.

Vijayendra Hariyal works as a global executive manager with an MNC. His first book, *Pursuit of Goodness*, written on lives of seven social entrepreneurs is now available for free to everyone who joins volstreet. com. He has also contributed stories to *Chicken Soup for the Indian Romantic Soul*.

Zainab Sulaiman is a freelance writer and businesswoman — she makes children's quilts under the Fatcat label; and is a busy mother to two young children. She blogs on the simple joys, challenges and rewards of parenting at memoriesofchocolate.wordpress.com and can be reached at fatcatbangalore@yahoo.com.

Permissions

Dowry Dilemma. Reprinted by permission of Parul Gupta. © 2010 Parul Gupta.

Fairytale Bride. Reprinted by permission of Shashi Agarwal. © 2010 Shashi Agarwal.

I Do. Reprinted by permission of Mariya Salim. © 2010 Mariya Salim.

Opposites Attract. Reprinted by permission of Monisha Sen. © 2010 Monisha Sen.

Slow Down … Please! Reprinted by permission of Vijayendra Haryal. © 2010 Vijayendra Haryal.

The Blushing Groom. Reprinted by permission of Shashi Agarwal. © 2010 Shashi Agarwal.

The Saint. Reprinted by permission of Rana Siddiqui Zaman. © 2010 Rana Siddiqui Zaman.

To Be with the One You Love. Reprinted by permission of Vibha Karnik. © 2010 Vibha Karnik.

We Are Married and We Still Date. Reprinted by permission of Hema Dhawan. © 2010 Hema Dhawan.